Lifers

Irwin writes about prisons from an unusual academic perspective. Before receiving a PhD in sociology, he served five years in a California state penitentiary for armed robbery. This is his sixth book on imprisonment—an ethnography of prisoners who have served more than 20 years in a California correctional institution. The purpose of the book is to take issue with the conventional wisdom on homicide, society's purposes of imprisonment, and offenders' reformability. Through the lifers' stories, Irwin reveals what happens to prisoners serving very long sentences in correctional facilities and what this should tell us about effective sentencing policy.

John Irwin taught sociology at San Francisco State University for 27 years, during which time he studied prisons and jails. His research was published in five books. He was also a member of the Working Party for the American Friends Service Committee that wrote the influential report *The Struggle for Justice*. He worked closely with the California legislature on the Uniform Sentencing Act passed in 1976.

CRIMINOLOGY AND JUSTICE STUDIES SERIES

Series Editors: **Chester Britt**, *Northeastern University*, **Shaun L. Gabbidon**, *Penn State Harrisburg*, and **Nancy Rodriguez**, *Arizona State University*

Criminology and Justice Studies offers works that make both intellectual and stylistic innovations in the study of crime and criminal justice. The goal of the series is to publish works that model the best scholarship and thinking in the criminology and criminal justice field today, but in a style that connects that scholarship to a wider audience including advanced undergraduates, graduate students, and the general public. The works in this series help fill the gap between academic monographs and encyclopedic textbooks by making innovative scholarship accessible to a large audience without the superficiality of many texts.

BOOKS IN THE SERIES

Published:
Biosocial Criminology
Edited by Anthony Walsh and Kevin M. Beaver

Community Policing in America
Jeremy M. Wilson

Criminal Justice Theory
Edited by David E. Duffee and Edward R. Maguire

Criminological Perspectives on Race and Crime
Shaun L. Gabbidon

Race, Law and American Society: 1607 to Present
Gloria J. Browne-Marshall

Today's White Collar Crime
Hank J. Brightman

White Collar Crime and Opportunity
Michael Benson and Sally Simpson

Forthcoming:
Crime and the Lifecourse
Michael Benson and Alex Piquero

Criminological Perspectives on Race and Crime, 2nd Edition
Shaun L. Gabbidon

Structural Equations Modeling for Criminology and Criminal Justice
George Higgins

Lifers

Seeking Redemption in Prison

John Irwin

Routledge
Taylor & Francis Group

NEW YORK AND LONDON

First published 2009
by Routledge
270 Madison Ave, New York, NY 10016

Simultaneously published in the UK
by Routledge
2 Park Square, Milton Park, Abingdon, Oxon OX14 4RN

Routledge is an imprint of the Taylor & Francis Group, an informa business

Typeset in Minion by
RefineCatch Limited, Bungay, Suffolk
Printed and bound in the United States of America on acid-free paper by
Walsworth Publishing Company, Marceline, MO

Library of Congress Cataloging-in-Publication Data
Irwin, John, 1929–
    Lifers : seeking redemption in prison / John Irwin.
        p. cm.—(Criminology and justice studies series)
    1. Prisoners—United States—Attitudes.   2. Prisoners—United States—Conduct of
life.   3. Criminals—Rehabilitation—United States.   4. Prisons—United States.   I. Title.
    HV9471.I776 2008
    365'.4—dc22

                                                                                    2009008560

ISBN10: 0–415–80168–0 (hbk)
ISBN10: 0–415–80198–2 (pbk)
ISBN10: 0–203–87622–9 (ebk)

ISBN13: 978–0–415–80168–3 (hbk)
ISBN13: 978–0–415–80198–0 (pbk)
ISBN13: 978–0–203–87622–0 (ebk)

CONTENTS

SERIES FOREWORD

Criminology and Justice Studies offers works that make both intellectual and stylistic innovations in the study of crime and criminal justice. The goal of the series is to publish works that model the best scholarship and thinking in the field today, but in a style that connects that scholarship to a wider audience including advanced undergraduates, graduate students, and the general public. The works in the series help fill the gap between academic monographs and encyclopedic textbooks by making innovative scholarship accessible to a large audience without the superficiality of many texts.

By a stroke of luck, Professor John Irwin selected our series for his latest treatise on American corrections, *Lifers*. In this important work, he provides readers with detailed insights into the lives of 17 lifers in California's notorious San Quentin prison. The backgrounds and experiences of the lifers show both the diversity and similarities of their lived experiences. As usual, Irwin's deep understanding of American corrections provides the context for a better understanding of the changing nature of sentencing that has produced record numbers of lifers. In addition, his work shows the humanity of the inmates, which is in stark contrast to the often demonic portrait of lifers. *Lifers* also points to the imperfection of the criminal justice system by highlighting the fact that one of the lifers was released because he was wrongly convicted. An additional theme of Irwin's text is a review of the enormous challenges facing lifers once they reenter society. In short, this book represents another key work by Professor Irwin. We can only hope students of the discipline will continue to take heed of Dr. Irwin's keen insights on this critical issue facing American society.

Chester Britt
Shaun L. Gabbidon
Nancy Rodriguez

PREFACE

Twenty-five years of a "tough on crime" policy have resulted in an explosion of our prison populations, which have gone from 196,000 in 1970 to over 1.5 million today. Within this general expansion, the proportion of persons serving terms with a life maximum (usually for first or second degree homicide) has increased. Short termers come and go, lifers accumulate. At present in California, which is the focus of this study, lifers are 15 percent of the population. What has happened is that in addition to more lifers being sent to prison, they serve much longer sentences.

I became interested in the lifer situation when I was completing a study of prisoner social organization in the California State Prison at Solano. I moved my focus to San Quentin and began interviewing lifers and attending the self-help programs they had organized. I discovered that many of the public's ideas about homicide, lifers, their crimes, their prison "careers," and their threat to society if released are distorted or mistaken. This book attempts to correct these misunderstandings and present an accurate portrayal of lifers' pre-prison lives, crimes, maturation, and transformation in prison. The major conclusion of the study is that whoever these lifers were or whatever crime they committed, the vast majority of them become decent persons after serving years in prison.

My original interest was stimulated by my discovery at Solano State Prison of (1) how much time lifers were currently serving and (2) how the parole board and the governor were going against the sentencing laws of the state and denying parole to almost all prisoners who were eligible for release. So the book also examines the lifers' legal predicament. The sentencing law that was passed in 1976 instructed the Department of Corrections to set guidelines for sentencing lifers who are eligible for release. It also stipulates that the parole board "shall normally" set the prisoners' parole date according to these guidelines unless there is evidence that the prisoners, if released, will be a future threat to public safety. Until 1985, the parole board followed these legal procedures and prisoners convicted of first degree homicide were serving an average of about 12 years, a sentence length that had been the same since the 1950s. Then the punitive movement reached its full force. Lifers became defined as repudiated pariah and their sentences leaped up. The California parole board began denying parole to almost all lifers on the basis that their crime revealed that they would be a future danger to society and releases of lifers shut down to a trickle. Lifers' sentences doubled or tripled with many serving over 30 years.

California prisoners have waged a lengthy battle in the courts against the current sentencing practices and it appears that they are about to win. If that happens, a flood of lifers will be released. This eventuality is discussed in the final chapter.

ACKNOWLEDGMENTS

I must give primary credit to the many prisoners serving life terms who made this study possible and to whom it is dedicated. Marvin Mutch, who has served 33 years for a crime for which he was convicted on scant circumstantial evidence and appears to be innocent, assisted me at every stage of the research and in the writing of the manuscript. Mr. Mutch helped me contact the lifers I interviewed, discussed all the ideas in the book as they were taking shape, and read and commented on drafts of the emerging manuscript. The other 16 lifers allowed me to interview them and also read at least parts of the manuscript and gave me feedback that contributed to my work. They are Bobby Brown, John Dannenberg, Julius Domantay, Jerry Elster, Willy (Rachman) Green, Albert Losno, Lonnie Morris, Richard Pomo, Shahid Roufe, Vince Russo, P. J. Seiler, Bryan Smith, Watani Steiner, Russel Trunzo, Noel Valdivia, and German Yambao. During the study I was in regular contact with many other lifers who provided me with information related to my study. James Carlin, Paul Jordan, Steven Lieb, Hector Oropeza, Wayne Reynolds, and Curtis Roberts are among them.

Many members of the staff at San Quentin aided my research. Deputy Warden Max Lemon gave me initial approval to continue my studies of California prisoners at San Quentin. Associate Warden J. C. Allen was very helpful at some crucial points in the study. Laura Bowman was most cooperative as were Pastor Morris Curry, Iman R. S. Hassan, and Rabbi C. Hyman.

Michael Snedeker, who has helped me in earlier studies, particularly *Prisons in Turmoil*, came to my assistance with crucial suggestions, editing, and even a paragraph or two. James Austin supplied me with important data on lifers. My wife Marsha Rosenbaum, as always, read my drafts and made excellent suggestions. Jody Lewen, who originally invited me to come to San Quentin, which led to my undertaking of the study of lifers, read a draft and made suggestions.

1

INTRODUCTION

While I was studying Solano State Prison (2000 to 2004), I drew together a group of convict "experts" to supply me with information about prisoner behavior patterns and prisoner social organization and to critique drafts of the chapters I wrote.[1] It turned out that all my experts were "lifers," most of them in prison for homicide.[2] They had all served in excess of 20 years. Through my extended association with them, I was convinced that they were intelligent, sincere, and decent human beings. In addition, I became aware of their circumstances, particularly the difficulty they were having in obtaining a parole. I knew from my former experiences with the California prison system that before 1975, persons convicted of first degree homicide served an average of 12 to 13 years. What these shorter sentences for the most serious crimes reflect is that society in the decades before 1980 demanded less punishment for crimes *and* believed that offenders were redeemable.

It became clear to me that in this punitive era in penology most people—particularly government functionaries, prison employees, and parole board members—view lifers as repudiated pariah and are extremely reluctant to allow their release on parole. This is reflected in

---

1   This study is published in a book titled *The Warehouse Prison: Disposal of the New Dangerous Class* (New York: Oxford University Press, 2005).

2   It is natural that the experts were lifers. Lifers tend to know more about the prison and prisoner social organization than "short termers" and are more willing to engage in a protracted study.

the public announcement California Governor Gray Davis made soon after taking office in 1999 that the only way a person convicted of homicide was going to get out of prison during his tenure was with a toe tag and in a bag—in other words, dead. Even most prison reformers ignore lifers and focus their efforts on petty drug offences or non-violent, unserious felonies. Over 1,000 persons convicted of first or second degree murder come to prison each year and there are over 10,000 who, according to the law and administrative regulations, are eligible for release. Only 230 have been released on parole in the last 10 years.[3]

The truth is that whoever they were and whatever crime they committed, the vast majority of lifers become completely different people after serving years in prison. Two things unavoidably happen to them. First, they are removed from the social contexts that in many complicated ways influenced their orientation, values, and viewpoints and contributed to their crimes. Second, they mature. Beyond these two inevitable changes, most of them consciously undertake a transformation of their thinking, orientation, and personality. This leads to their actively taking advantage of every resource available to prepare themselves for a different life when they are released. Not only do they prepare themselves through education and vocational training, they actively and collectively seek atonement and, perhaps, even redemption through a multitude of programs, most of which they, the prisoners themselves, organized and maintain.

Because of the changes they experience, most California lifers are transformed into persons who pose a minimal threat to public safety.[4] In fact, they become conscientious and decent individuals who can, given the chance, make valuable contributions to society. However, because of the seriousness of the crimes (usually homicides) they committed 25 or more years earlier, they continue to be viewed and processed as dangerous criminals.

This practice of holding lifers 10 to 15 years beyond the time prescribed by the law and formally established administrative policy is unjust and, apparently, as California and Federal Courts have recently been ruling, illegal.[5] Also, it is financially disastrous. The California prison system is experiencing extreme overcrowding and fiscal

---

3 Data come from California Department of Corrections and Rehabilitation Web site: www.cdcr.ca.gov.

4 According to the statistics gathered by U.S. Department of Justice, Bureau of Justice Statistics, 1.2% of persons convicted of homicide commit another homicide after release. Only 10.8% are returned to prison with a new felony conviction. This is the lowest recidivism rate of all felons.

5 Chapter 6 examines the legal status of sentencing practices in California.

problems. It has the largest population in the country. Though it built 22 new prisons in the 1980s and 1990s, each now holding 6,000 prisoners, it is at 170 percent capacity. Three Federal Judges are currently holding hearings on a lawsuit regarding this overcrowding. Also, its medical delivery system is being monitored by the Federal Court, which has ruled that it is in violation of U.S. Constitutional cruel and unusual treatment standards.

Aging lifers become more and more expensive to take care of in prison. Kara Dansky, the executive director of the Stanford Criminal Justice Center, has calculated the added cost of aging prisoners, as this article explains:

> Without a considerable boost in funding, the prospect of prisons accommodating older prisoners properly will remain bleak. Part of the problem is that caring for these aging and elderly inmates is incredibly expensive, says Kara Dansky, a lawyer and the executive director of the Stanford Criminal Justice Center. She estimates California spends about $43,000 annually to incarcerate an inmate. But national studies show that older inmates—who are more likely to have medical conditions like diabetes or heart disease—cost at least an additional $25,000.
>
> Some of those added costs are for medical services, while others are for equipment. An August 2007 report commissioned by the medical receiver of the state prison system said the state needs 3,224 medical beds now (it has approximately 800) and will need 5,292 by 2017 if the older-inmate population continues to grow at the current pace. The legislative analyst's office estimates that construction of proposed new medical facilities could cost the state as much as $3 billion.[6]

In effect, the "tough on crime," movement has California government officials backed into a corner. The movement has resulted in massive prison overcrowding and an array of attendant problems, one of which is the growing population of lifers who become the most costly prisoners. However, these officials—the governor, legislators, Supreme Court justices, and parole board members—are either committed to being tough on crime or are fearful of being seen as soft on crime and are, therefore, unwilling to take steps to solve these problems. Solving them would require, above all, shortening prison sentences and this they are unwilling to do.

---

6   Sarah Arnquist, "Aging Behind Bars," *California Lawyer* (May 2008), p. 11.

MY STUDY

In 2006 I began associating with and interviewing lifers housed at San Quentin. I eventually completed long interviews of 17 lifers. I did not select these persons according to a systematic sampling procedure. I merely interviewed persons whom I got to know and who were willing to be interviewed. Since I wanted to focus on people who had served long sentences, I only interviewed persons who had served at least 20 years. In addition, I circulated in the prison, got to know dozens of lifers, and attended many meetings of the various programs in which they were involved.

My own biography equips me to understand and evaluate their criminal past, prison experiences, and conversion. I am intimately familiar with all these aspects of their lives. I can sincerely state, there but by the twists of fate go I. At the age of 16, I started stealing car parts, then cars, in order to build my own "roadster."[7] I progressed to safe burglary and then armed robbery with considerable drug use thrown in. In this journey to prison, I acquired a complete criminal identity. I was sent to prison for armed robbery with a sentence of 5 to life and served 5 years. On the last robbery my crime partner and I committed, a "shootout" ensued. The owner of the business we were robbing came through a side door firing a .45 at my partner. While dashing out of the building, my partner returned a pistol round in the general direction of the owner. The owner proceeded to fire at us while we rapidly departed in a stolen car. Luck was on our side and nobody was killed. If someone had been, we would have been guilty of "felony murder," a capital offense.

In prison I prepared myself for a different career. Upon release, I went to college, eventually receiving a PhD in sociology. The subject of my dissertation was the career of the felon and it took me back to the prison to study convicts. The dissertation was published in a widely read book—*The Felon*. I then began my career as a college professor and continued studying incarceration.[8] In addition to conducting studies of prisoners, I pursued prison reform and prisoner rehabilitation. For 50 years, my close contact with prisoners and ex-prisoners has been

---

7 A "roadster," a California creation, was usually a Model A or 1932 Ford convertible with the fenders and bumpers stripped off and equipped with a "hopped up" motor, and special wheels and tires. It later was called a "rod" or "hot rod."

8 In addition to *The Felon* (Berkeley, CA: University of California Press, 1970), I wrote *Prisons in Turmoil* (Boston: Little, Brown, 1980), *The Jail* (Berkeley, CA: University of California Press, 1985), with James Austin, *It's About Time* (Belmont, CA: Wadsworth, 1990), and *The Warehouse Prison*, cited previously.

broad and constant. I fully understand and appreciate their transformation in prison.

The primary data of my study are long interviews of the 17 lifers I selected for the study. As indicated above, these lifers had all served more than 20 years for first degree, or second degree homicide, attempted homicide, or conspiracy to commit homicide. They had served years beyond the minimum recommended by sentencing law and prison administrative policy. My examination of their prison careers led to my conclusions on the transformation they experience while serving their long sentences. In an attempt to reveal to readers essential information about the lifers' early lives and the nature of their transformations, I have included lengthy quotes from the interviews, which were recorded and transcribed. It is my intention that, through the lifers' disclosures, the reader will form an understanding of these men and their transformation.

My primary purpose in writing this book is to demonstrate that most lifers are not fundamentally evil people and that over time they become trustworthy and conscientious individuals who pose no threat to public safety. In fact, most of them desire to engage in social services upon their release. I also argue that holding lifers for years beyond their prescribed sentences has severe negative consequences, the most obvious being the enormous added expense of their incarceration. But also, it is cruel and unjust to punish people more than is required to fulfill society's desire for retribution for their crimes. Through a lengthy series of changes in sentencing laws and administrative rules, the California Legislature and the Department of Corrections established the appropriate punishment for various forms of homicide. The final product came *after* the "tough on crime" movement swept the nation and is, therefore, relatively punitive.

In addition to retribution, the official purposes of imprisonment include general deterrence, incapacitation, and rehabilitation. How much punishment is required to deter other citizens from breaking the law is difficult to determine and remains controversial. Many students of criminal justice agree that most citizens are deterred by the threat of punishment by the government. However, there is considerable agreement that the deterrence value does not continue to increase with increases in punishment.[9] Lifers in California serve many more years than is justified by society's need to deter others from committing crime.

---

9   See Working Party for the American Friends Service Committee, *The Struggle for Justice* (New York: Hill and Wang, 1971) for a discussion of general deterrence.

Nor is it fair or rational to keep lifers for years and years in order to incapacitate them because it is feared that they pose an ongoing threat to public safety. Some of them, particularly some young males, would be a threat if they were released in a short time. But maturity and other processes they pass through during imprisonment convert lifers into non-violent and non-criminal individuals. Only 1.2 percent commit another homicide after release. (We will see in Chapter 6 how the California parole board and the governor generally disregard the punishment standards set by the law and administrative policy and invoke incapacitation as a justification to hold lifers for longer periods.)

It must be noted that California has never completely abandoned rehabilitation as a purpose of imprisonment and has recently reemphasized it by adding "rehabilitation" to the name of the prison system—"The Department of Corrections and Rehabilitation." As you will see, the lifers I studied demonstrate, to the extreme, the fulfillment of rehabilitation.

THE LIFER SITUATION IN CALIFORNIA

While California's prison population exploded (from about 50,000 in 1980 to 175,000 in 2007), the proportion of prisoners serving life sentences grew even more rapidly. This is because more people are being sent to prison for life sentences and they are serving longer and longer prison terms. Short termers come and go. Lifers accumulate. As of January 1, 2007, there were 25,379 prisoners serving life sentences in California prisons. These include persons serving 7 to life (the sentence for first degree homicide prior to 1978), 15 to life (the current sentence for second degree homicide and kidnap with robbery), 25 to life (the sentence for first degree homicide or for a "third strike"—a third felony conviction following conviction for two prior convictions for "serious felonies"), and life without possibility of parole (the sentence for first degree homicide with special circumstances). African Americans were 32% of the total, Latinos 34%, and white prisoners 25%. Ninety percent of these lifers had no prior felony conviction.

Since the decades before the 1980s, lifers' sentences have more than doubled. This great increase was one of the consequences of the "tough on crime" movement that arose in the late 1970s and gained momentum through the 1980s and 1990s. As pointed out above, Governor Davis announced that lifers in prison for homicide would serve their entire life in prison. Since the California governor has veto power over all parole decisions for persons charged with homicide, a power given the governor through a California referendum passed in

1988, Davis was almost able to fulfill his promise. He allowed only six persons guilty of homicide to be released in the five years he was governor. The governor before Davis, Pete Wilson, who started the policy of denying lifers parole, released only 123 in his eight years in office. Arnold Schwarzenegger released over 100 in his first two years as governor. But then, as his reelection approached, he slowed down. Now he has turned to a policy more like that of Gray Davis. In the first half of 2007, he signed off on only four.

In California, as in most states in the U.S., lifers' sentences are very long compared to other countries and to prior decades in California itself. For example, according to a survey conducted for the Bureau of Justice Statistics in 2004, in the U.S. persons served 21 years for homicide.[10] In Sweden they served 4 years, Switzerland 5 years, Netherlands 9.5 years, Scotland 8.8 years, Canada 10.6 years, Australia 11 years, and England and Wales 17 years.[11]

California, compared to other states in the U.S., is not outstanding in the length of sentence lifers must serve. In six states—Illinois, Iowa, Louisiana, Maine, Pennsylvania, and South Dakota—life is life. To be released, lifers in these states must have their sentences commuted by the governor. In 1992, Michigan passed a law that mandated that lifers serve at least 15 years and since then the parole board has been following a "life means life" policy.[12]

In California, prior to 1985 and changes in sentencing laws and the rise of a punitive national movement, persons sentenced for first degree murder served an average of 12 years (see Table 1.1). This average was relatively constant between 1945 and 1985, after which it zoomed upward.

Though the number released each year was creeping upward, about 42 persons were released each year. Between 1945 and 1949, 169 were released and between 1980 and 1984, 212 were released.[13] During the terms of Governors Wilson, Davis, and Schwarzenegger all prisoners

---

10 This figure is lower than actual sentences because it is based on time served by prisoners released in a certain time period. When sentences are increasing, which was the case in 2004, persons serving the more recent longer sentences are underrepresented in release cohorts.

11 David P. Farrington, Patrick A. Langan, and Michael Tonry, *Cross-National Studies in Crime and Justice* (Washington, DC: U.S. Department of Justice, September 2004). These cross-national rates are for all types of homicides, which may include manslaughter that in the U.S. would not receive a life sentence.

12 See Marc Mauer, Ryan S. King, and Malcolm C. Young, *The Meaning of "Life": Long Prison Sentences in Context* (Washington, DC: The Sentencing Project, 2004), pp. 3–8.

13 These data come from the Office of Research, California Department of Corrections and Rehabilitation.

Table 1.1
Average sentences for first degree homicide in California

1945–1949	1950–1954	1955–1959	1960–1964	1965–1969	1970–1974	1975–1979	1980–1984
14 years	12 years	11 years	11.5 years	11.5 years	11.7 years	11 years	11.9 years

sentenced to prison for first degree murder who were given paroles served over 20 years.

The most revealing comparison is between lifers' current sentences and the time served by persons who were sentenced to death in California and had their sentences automatically commuted to life when, in 1972, the Supreme Court of the United States overturned all death penalties because they were ruled to have been discriminatorily determined. Nineteen California prisoners who had their sentences commuted and were subsequently released on parole, served an average of 13.9 years. Four of the nineteen were sent to prison before 1968 and could not serve this low average. If we removed them from the calculation, the remaining 15 persons served an average of 12.8 years.

These persons were not convicted of relatively less than average serious murders, such as being the driver in an armed robbery that resulted in a homicide. For example, while Robert Nye was burglarizing a residence, the woman resident grabbed a knife from the kitchen to protect herself. Nye wrestled the knife from her and stabbed her 39 times. He served 12 years. Terry Mabry shot and killed a police officer who had gone to his house with other policemen to arrest Mabry for armed robberies he had committed. He served 14 years.

What these shorter sentences for the most serious crimes reflect is that the society in the decades before 1980 demanded less punishment for crimes *and* believed that offenders were redeemable.

Several changes and developments that occurred after 1975 caused the dramatic escalation of lifers' sentences. The first of these was a national shift in sentencing philosophy away from rehabilitation. In the late 1960s and early 1970s, many progressive criminologists, prisoner activists (myself included), and prisoner support organizations were disillusioned with the operation of prison systems in which release decisions were based on rehabilitative criteria.[14] We were particularly

---

14 See American Friends Service Committee, *The Struggle for Justice*, which was the first of a series of books written by scholars critical of the operation of the rehabilitative ideal.

critical of the indeterminate sentence systems within which parole boards had large margins of discretion. These critics believed that, since there were no reliable rehabilitative strategies or methods to determine when someone had been rehabilitated, parole boards were deciding sentences by unacceptable, perhaps unconstitutional, criteria. This "arbitrary" decision-making resulted in unacceptable disparities in sentences and some unusually long sentences for particular individuals. This determinate sentencing movement succeeded in establishing "uniform" sentencing based on crime seriousness. It was the original intent of the critics of indeterminate sentencing that shorter, uniform sentences that corresponded to the seriousness of the crime be delivered. However, as states such as California shifted to uniform sentencing, conservative legislators moved swiftly to emphasize the punishment spirit of the new laws and caused sentences to become longer and longer under the new sentencing approach. As I wrote regarding this movement in 1980:

> conservative legislators attached themselves to the issue. Making political currency out of the public's fear of street crime and bringing considerable public attention to the bills, these legislators succeeded in cowering uncommitted or ambivalent colleagues.[15]

California passed the Uniform Sentencing Act in January 1977. It established four categories of crimes and each category gave the judge three different sentences: for example, two, four, or six years for burglary. The judge could "enhance" a sentence for prior convictions, weapon possession, weapon use, and multiple offenses. However, by the time the law came into effect in July 1976, the designated sentences had already been increased and continued to be regularly increased by legislators who had joined a "tough on crime" movement that was sweeping the country. What started as a system to keep sentences uniform and relatively short, became a highly punitive one with great margins of discretion for judges and prosecutors (particularly prosecutors) to vary sentences for similar crimes.

More important for our concern, the authors of the Uniform Sentencing Act failed to deal with several crimes that at the time carried life sentences. These were first and second degree homicide; attempted homicide; kidnap with ransom, reward, extortion, rape, robbery or physical injury; train wrecking; and assault on a prison guard. In the case of these crimes, the prisoner would make his or her first board appearance after serving seven years and was eligible

---

15 Irwin, *Prisons in Turmoil*, p. 226.

for parole at that time. The sentence for these crimes came to be referred to as "7 to life."

In the early years of the operation of the new sentencing system, the spirit of uniformity and to some degree restraint in the delivery of excessive punishment guided lawmakers and paroling authorities in determining lifers' sentences. The law passed in 1978 that guided the determination of lifers' sentences reads:

> The Board of Prison Terms shall meet with each inmate during the third year of incarceration for the purposes of reviewing the inmate's file, making recommendations, and documenting activities and conduct pertinent to granting or withholding post conviction credit. One year prior to the inmate's minimum eligible parole release date a panel of two or more commissioners or deputy commissioners shall again meet with the inmate and *shall normally* set a parole release date as provided in Section 3041. (Emphasis added.)

This law, PC 3041, instructed the parole board to achieve uniformity in sentencing and to establish criteria for setting parole dates:

> The release date shall be set in a manner that will provide uniform terms for offenses of similar gravity and magnitude in respect to their threat to the public, and that will comply with sentencing rules that the Judicial Council may issue and any sentencing information relevant to the setting of parole release dates. The board shall establish criteria for the setting of parole release dates and in doing so shall consider the number of victims of the crime for which the inmate was sentenced and other factors in mitigation or aggravation of the crime.

In 1975, under the indeterminate sentencing system, the parole board established a matrix to guide the parole board in setting sentences for first degree murder (see Table 1.2).

After 1977 and the passage of the Uniform Sentencing Act, new matrices were established (see Tables 1.3 and 1.4). (The sentences in the new matrices were considerably longer.)

From 1977 to 1985, the parole board obeyed the spirit of the law and followed the matrices in setting lifers' sentences. This is reflected in the average sentence for first degree murder given from 1975 to 1985, which was 11.5 years, about the same that it had been for two decades. Also, 80 percent of these sentences were between 7.3 and 17 years, which reflects considerable uniformity in sentencing.

After 1985, sentencing practices changed dramatically. What

Table 1.2
Matrix of base terms for first degree murder committed before January 1, 1979

	A. Indirect	B. Direct	C. Severe Trauma	D. Torture
I. Participating Victim Victim was an accomplice or otherwise implicated in a criminal act with the prisoner during which or as a result of which the death occurred	8-10-12	10-12-14	11-13-15	13-15-17
II. Prior Relationship Victim was involved in a personal relationship with prisoner (spouse, family member friend, etc.) which contributed to the motivation for the act resulting in death. If victim had a personal relationship but prisoner hired and/or paid a person to commit the offense	10-12-14	12-14-16	13-15-17	15-17-19
III. No Prior Relationship Victim had little or no personal relationship with prisoner; or motivation for act resulting in death was related to accomplishment of another crime; e.g. death of victim during robbery, rape, or other felony	11-13-15	13-15-17	14-16-18	16-18-20
IV. Threat to Public Order or Murder for Hire The act resulting in the victim's death constituted a threat to the public order. Include murder of a police officer, prison guard, public official, fellow patient or prisoner, and killing within an institution or any killing where the prisoner hired and/or paid another person to commit the murder of the victim	13-15-17	15-17-19	16-18-20	18-20-22

intervened was the punitive movement driven by the fear of crime that was stirred up by politicians, media spokespersons, and some conservative social scientists. A key and revealing event in this movement, which sent reverberations across the country, was the use by George Bush Sr.'s campaign of the rape committed by a convict whom one of

Table 1.3
Matrix of base terms for first degree murder committed after November 8, 1978

	A. Indirect	B. Direct	C. Severe Trauma	D. Torture
I. Participating Victim Victim was an accomplice or otherwise implicated in a criminal act with the prisoner during which or as a result of which the death occurred	25-26-27	26-27-28	27-28-29	28-29-30
II. Prior Relationship Victim was involved in a personal relationship with prisoner (spouse, family member friend, etc.) which contributed to the motivation for the act resulting in death. If victim had a personal relationship but prisoner hired and/or paid a person to commit the offense	26-27-28	27-28-29	28-29-30	29-30-31
III. No Prior Relationship Victim had little or no personal relationship with prisoner; or motivation for act resulting in death was related to accomplishment of another crime; e.g. death of victim during robbery, rape, or other felony	27-28-29	28-29-30	29-30-31	30-31-32
IV. Threat to Public Order or Murder for Hire The act resulting in the victim's death constituted a threat to the public order. Include murder of a police officer, prison guard, public official, fellow patient or prisoner, and killing within an institution or any killing where the prisoner hired and/or paid another person to commit the murder of the victim.	28-29-30	29-30-31	30-31-32	31-32-33

the campaign workers referred to as "a big black rapist."[16] Willy Horton committed a rape while on a short furlough from prison through a

---

16 For a more complete description of this incident see Katherine Beckett, quoted in Kenneth Karst, *Law's Promise, Law's Expression: Visions of Power in the Politics of Race, Gender, and Religion* (New Haven, CT: Yale University Press, 1993), pp. 73–74.

Table 1.4
Matrix of base terms for second degree murder committed after November 8, 1978

	A. Indirect	B. Direct	C. Severe Trauma
I. Participating Victim Victim was an accomplice or otherwise implicated in a criminal act with the prisoner during which or as a result of which the death occurred	15-16-17	16-17-18	17-18-19
II. Prior Relationship Victim was involved in a personal relationship with prisoner (spouse, family member friend, etc.) which contributed to the motivation for the act resulting in death. If victim had a personal relationship but prisoner hired and/or paid a person to commit the offense	16-17-18	17-18-19	18-19-20
III. No Prior Relationship Victim had little or no personal relationship with prisoner; or motivation for act resulting in death was related to accomplishment of another crime; e.g. death of victim during robbery, rape, or other felony	17-18-19	18-19-20	19-20-21

work release program. George Bush was running behind Michael Dukakis in the polls. Members of Bush's campaign team searched for a person released from prison during Dukakis' tenure as governor of Massachusetts and found Willy Horton. Though hundreds of prisoners had received work furloughs during the same period and Dukakis had nothing directly to do with Horton's release, the Bush campaign was able to frighten the public with the possibility that rapists, and black rapists to boot, were being released from prison early and to blame Dukakis for the release. Bush swung ahead in the polls and won the election.

The new punitive spirit prevailed and the California parole board and governor began turning down or vetoing the release of lifers who, by the standards set in the law and by all rehabilitative criteria, were eligible for parole. Wilson, governor from 1991 to 1999, began the slowdown, Davis virtually ceased releasing lifers, and Schwarzenegger, after releasing slightly over 100 in his first two years, has slowed the release down to a small trickle. What is happening is that thousands of lifers are accumulating in prison even though they have served almost twice the time called for by the matrices. This is happening in spite of the fact that they have spent years participating in academic, vocational training, and self-help rehabilitative programs, many of which they created themselves. And in spite of the fact that they are increasingly posing a huge medical care problem for the prison system, which is under court receivership because of its inadequate medical care system. The Dukakis syndrome is another factor influencing sentencing decision-making. All politicians who face reelection worry about being singled out as an individual who was responsible for the release of a prisoner who committed serious crimes, particularly rape or murder. This explains Schwarzenegger's shift in practices. He became unpopular soon after his victory in the Governor Davis recall election because he tried and failed to push through a set of public referendums that involved expensive projects and massive reorganization of government. He radically changed many of his policies. One was his plan to revamp the prison system by shifting to rehabilitation, reducing prison populations, and releasing more lifers who were stacking up in the prison. His advisers persuaded him to back away from prison reform and slow down releasing lifers.

The actions of victims' rights organizations added force to the Dukakis syndrome. In California, Crime Victims United, an organization largely funded by the California Correctional Peace Officers Association (CCPOA), regularly testifies before government committees, encourages victims to appear at parole board hearings of prisoners involved in crimes related to the victims' victimization, *and* campaigns against politicians whom they define as soft on crime. Needless to say, this and other similar groups have considerable influence over public opinion. Politicians who are considering reelection carefully avoid their disapproval.

In moving away from the sentencing practices that prevailed before 1985, parole board members, governors, and judges who review governors' and parole board members' decisions have moved from one theory of crime and criminals to another. In the earlier period, the decades preceding 1985, penologists and criminal justice functionaries were guided by the "rehabilitative ideal." The view of criminals within this penological theory is that their criminality is a result of social and psychological factors and that through treatment methods criminals can be "rehabilitated." In the current theory, criminals are viewed as being fundamentally different from conventional people and their criminality is deeply rooted in their make-up. They are, in the words of James Q. Wilson, the social scientist who promoted this new penological perspective in his popular book, *Thinking About Crime*, "wicked people."[17]

* * *

In the following four chapters, the 17 lifers' early lives, crimes, and transformations will be examined. Special attention will be paid to the nature of "typical" homicides and to the misconceptions regarding homicide held by the public. In Chapter 6, the lifers' legal predicament will be studied. Finally, an Epilogue will explore developments that appear to be unfolding because of changes in the law that will result in the release of many, perhaps hundreds, of lifers.

---

17 James Q. Wilson, *Thinking About Crime* (New York: Random House, 1975), p. 235. See also by Wilson, "Lock 'Em Up," *New York Times Magazine*, March 9, 1975, p. 11.

2

THE LIFERS

Nine of the seventeen lifers were raised on society's margins. They are non-white sons of immigrants or poor African-American families, some of which were dysfunctional. Two were born in the Philippines and came to the United States when they were 9 and 11 years old. Two finished high school, but the others dropped out by the age of 16. They all were in close contact with other marginal people who were involved in regular "deviant" activity—drug use, "gangbanging," and stealing. Violence was all around them. They started close to the edge and it didn't take much for them to tumble over it.

Albert

Albert had a better start than the others. His father immigrated from Lima, Peru, his mother from Guayaquil, Ecuador. They came to the United States before Albert was born. His family life was stable until his father left. Then Albert moved back and forth between his father's home in the East Bay and his mother's in San Francisco:

> I was born in San Francisco, California, the Mission District, 1962. I come from a real good family. We had family disputes when we were growing up like every family—arguments. I grew up in a time when I was experiencing a lot of racism—1970s late '60s. My family split up. My father moved away. He left me and my brother. My brother was younger than me. Then he came back and tried to make amends and he promised us a better life if I'd go live with him in Oakland, California. I was about eight.

For a few years in Oakland, things went well for Albert. He and his brother lived with their father near Lake Merritt and Albert went to St. Anthony, then St. Elizabeth, good Catholic schools. They moved to San Lorenzo and Albert transferred to a public school where he experienced more discrimination and racial conflict than in the private schools. Also he missed the discipline and structure of Catholic schools. He dropped out of school and returned to San Francisco:

> What the hell. I just left. I went back to the city to stay. During that time, I was just floating around trying to see really, what am I going to do. I needed money. I had to work. I have a uncle who lived in LA at that time. Had his own pool table business. He offered me a job making pool tables. He paid me good money, so I went to LA for a about a year. Orange County, Santa Ana, as a matter of fact. Became homesick, came back to San Francisco. So I came back to San Francisco and that's where I eventually met Maria, who became the mother of my kid. And that's what really changed my life around where being a teenager you fall in love with your first girlfriend. She came into my world and I didn't want to leave her. We became inseparable.

Back in the San Francisco Mission District, he became part of a small clique of teenagers who became a "gang:"

> I also had a lot of friends living the lifestyle that I didn't really agree with. Nevertheless, I tried to live up to the expectations, to that image you had to carry. People call it gangs, but it was really a neighborhood clique that just hung around together from the same neighborhood. Coming from the Mission District, that is *the* neighborhood. It is the most popular one with the girls and things like that. So, we built our own super-hero characters, so to speak. I had to live up to that expectation. I end up running around with a group of guys, formed a little clique called "Little Park." Now we had to carry another reputation—the Little Park Gang. I experienced that lifestyle for a minute and noticed where it was going to lead to. I could kind of see it coming. It was going to get a little worse and worse. So I decided to fade away. When I say fade away, it was walk away from the gang. And I told the guys who formed the gang that I was no longer interested in the lifestyle. I didn't want to participate in the gang setting any more. We could still be friends, not to take it personally. I have my girlfriend now. She's pregnant. So I started working two jobs. I worked at Candlestick Park. I worked at a condominium in South San

Francisco. My responsibility became not only myself, but Maria, who was carrying my first daughter. That became my world. I became a man without knowing what it is to be a man. Losing my teenage innocence, trying to do the best I can.

When I dropped away from the gang, that's when my friends started using derogatory words, like you're pussy whipped, a mofo, a lame. I said, "I rather be pussy whipped knowing I'm waking up next to someone taking care of me, feeding me something, instead of waking up in alleyways, up in some staircase with my friends, malt liquor, smoking weed, knowing we are going to get up tomorrow, our breath stinking, waking up in some staircase just because I want to do it with my so called homeboys." Then if you want to call me pussy whipped because I'm spending time with a beautiful girl, then you can still say that I'm gone. But my relationship with them was high five, "How you doing everyone." I accepted a few rides to work or wherever. Until that day.

Bobby

Bobby, a black youth, grew up in the black ghettos of South Los Angeles:

I was raised in Watts in Los Angeles. I had a great family, mother and father was there. My father worked all the time. My mother, she was a housewife until I guess, until I was about eight years old. She started working. We moved from Watts in '69 and we moved to Compton and made Compton our first home in a big old house. Plenty of fun. I got four siblings: two brothers and two sisters. I'm the oldest boy. My sister is older than me.

I went to several schools. I had a lot of problems in school, I guess. A lot had to do with, maybe I didn't fit in, you know, name-calling and stuff like that. I fought a lot. I was an angry child. I was called a lot of names and there was a lot of racism. Some of the other schools that we had to call out our names so I ended up in a lot of fights. I got kicked out of school a couple times.

I got suspended when I was in, let me see, junior high. I think, my second year in junior high, got kicked out and I got suspended for two weeks for fighting. I hit a guy with a typewriter, yeah. But he hit me first, so I hit him with the typewriter. Mr. Keal was a vice principal. He got me by my collar one time and told me to wash my neck. I had got burned, hot water burn, when I was a kid and they left dark marks on my neck. And so I got upset and I swung at the vice principal and so I got suspended for that. So then from there I went to Dominquez High. It was pretty good. It was just, there we had a lot of neighborhood fights. I played hooky a lot, you know. It's probably the reason, because I didn't read too well. So I kinda felt, how do I say, embarrassed or something like that when the people ask me to read or something. To avoid that, I skipped school and so I ditched so I wouldn't be embarrassed. I got me a job around the 11th grade.

I was working for Martel and I did that for a while until somebody accused me of mixing plastic bits. They didn't like me there, I guess, and I got fired. So then I didn't go back to school. Later on, 16 years old, me and my father got into it and I got kicked out the house.

I went out on my own and I got my first apartment, me and a girl, got our first apartment. I was 16. She was 17 or 18. Got her pregnant, so we stayed together for about, up until I was 20.

He began experimenting with drugs at that time, mostly smoking marijuana, some of it laced with PCP, "angel dust." His girlfriend gave birth to a boy and Bobby got a job. Then they broke up and he began living in his car:

After that I had a son that was born, which made me grow up a lot faster. I started working at a car wash. I stayed there for a while at the car wash and me and the girl broke up. I didn't have a place to stay, so I just lived in my car. I was too proud to go ask my father if I can come back home. So I stayed out, slept in my car for a while and my car broke down and then I lost my job. So things started going downhill around 19 years of age and I know my mother told my father to go get me. So they brought me back home when I was 19 and we got along real well. We did pretty good and about when I was 20 years old, I got a job at Kimberly Clark, making diapers. And I was working there with my mother and things were looking up for me. Started building on the back room, which I was proud of, in my father's house.

After living back at home for a while, doing well, he began using cocaine. He caught his hand in a machine at work and was in the hospital for 20 days. He blames the accident on the cocaine he was using. He moved out of his parents' house, but had difficulty finding employment. He said that his inability to fill out job applications prevented him from obtaining work. He moved in with another woman and his cocaine use increased. For the next five years, he bounced around from girlfriend to girlfriend and job to job, used more cocaine, began freebasing cocaine, and had another child. His life "spiraled out of control:"

> Cocaine, freebase, so by then my life just spiraled out of control. Well my mother got sick and she died on me in '80, so in '82 really everything got out of control and so I used the drugs basically to drown my feelings and stuff. So by the time, 1984, I went to jail for grand theft person during the LA Olympics in Los Angeles. I thought it was a wake-up call for me to wake up and get out of it and try to get my life back together. So I get out of jail after spending 31 days for grand theft person and I end up getting back with my kids' mother and we tried to work it all out and everything. By '84, everything was looking pretty promising. So I got a job working with this agency, this video company where people were making videos for Walt Disney and it was pretty good. I figured that, in supporting my kids and stuff like that, it gave me initiative to live, you know, for you to survive and maintain a better life by working for them. By doing well at home, by, let's see, by '85 I was still messing around with cocaine. I used to bring it home to support my addiction and at the same time I would work to take my check and put it into the house to try and balance out that way.

German

German's family moved from the Philippines to San Francisco when he was nine years old. He spoke Tagalog and had considerable trouble adjusting to his new social settings, particularly school. After his father died, he moved to the Sunset District of San Francisco. Many other Asian immigrants, particularly ethnic Chinese who had fled Vietnam after the war and were in refugee camps in Singapore before immigrating to the U.S., live in the western part of San Francisco—the Sunset and Richmond districts, which were plagued with gangs of young Chinese and Vietnamese. In this milieu, German drifted into the streets and gangbanging:

> When I come to America I think it was the culture, the difference. At first, I couldn't speak English, but I spoke fluently within six months after arriving in San Francisco. And when I was grown, about 20 days prior to after getting to America or 30 days my dad passed away and he passed away in a company accident where he was working. It's a tanning company and we moved out of downtown Market Street on 8th Street. We moved to the Sunset District. My mother got compensated for my dad's death from the company.

When he entered junior high, he began having trouble with the Anglo and Chinese students who were the dominant groups in the Sunset District. He and a few other Philippine youth began getting into trouble:

> I was gettin' along pretty good at first and then when I got to junior high that's when things got out of line. I started using drugs. I went to A. P. Giannini in San Francisco in the Sunset District and then I ended up going to a boys' ranch for stealing cars and stuff. A couple times I was sentenced to the boys' ranch; Hidden Valley Ranch and then Log Cabin Ranch. I was getting in trouble often.
>
> I started getting involved in gangs maybe when I was about 14. I just started hanging out and stopped going to school and stealing, doing drugs and getting, you know, into the lifestyle.

Jerry

Jerry, a black man, grew up in South Central, Los Angeles. Though his parents were strict and the family tight knit, when he and his six siblings "got out of sight" of their strict mother, they ran loose with the other young kids in the neighborhood. He finished high school after some scrapes with the law. But eventually the violence on the streets of South Los Angeles snared him:

> It's East LA. It's east side of South Central, right off of Main and Broadway. Main is on the east side. It's on the borderline of east and west. Well for me, I grew up with strict parenting. But my parents couldn't go with me outside and with the young kids in the neighborhood, once I got out of sight of Mama, I did what I wanted to do. So with six others, four other boys and two girls, and pretty much just ran rampant, once we got out of the house, out of her sight. I want to say around like eight and nine, about nine years old. I was out there doing whatever I wanted to do almost and she wasn't around and that's the way I wanted to do. I wasn't that bad, you know, just being rambunctious.
>
> But I say I really got caught up with the gang scene and stuff around two years later. I got caught up and became associated with the Crips, grew up in that area with them. They had just started around the early '70s. They say '69. I don't remember all that. I was only six years old then and it wasn't like they are today, totally different make-up of what they are today. When they first started, they were just a bunch of youngsters, you know, just enjoying their little rebellion.

He began fighting a lot, but not with guns. When guns became part of the gang activities, Jerry tried to pull away from the scene:

> When the guns and all that stuff wasn't out there, we fought with sticks and chains and pipes and stuff like that—knives. Coming up, I did a whole lot of fighting. Like I said, right now them guys is quick to run and get guns. We didn't. We'd walk miles on the east side of Los Angeles all the way to the west side just to have a fight. But today, they got cars. They got sophisticated weaponry and stuff they're dealing with. And they get in an argument now, they tell me just soon as shoot you rather than stand out there toe to toe. That don't mean nothing no more. We took a lot pride in fist fighting and stuff. I didn't see it happen, but heard about the leader of the Crips gettin' killed, who was a friend of mine, who I thought was like a god. Though the guy that really started the Crips, name was Raymond Washington, he got killed four blocks from my house. I went around and seen his body laid out and that kind of put a whole new twist on it for me and the end of that gang thing. I tried to pull away from all that.

On his mother's insistence, he continued school until the 10th grade when he was arrested and was sent to a juvenile camp. When he was released, he left the state to live with his aunt. He finished high school and then returned to Los Angeles:

> I was 15 years old about 14 or 15. I was in 10th grade, just started the 10th grade. My mom made me go to school as long as I could keep up the pretense. I was cool. So I stayed in school all the way until I ended up catching a juvenile case. I stopped running with the gangs, but I started doing other little silly stuff, burglarizing houses and stealing stuff and ended up going to juvenile camp. And after I got out of the camp, it was like very difficult to catch up with the school thing, so I just made my mind up being I wasn't going to really do the school thing. So I left the state. I went and stayed with my auntie. And she demanded that I go back to school, so I went to school for a little while. I end up graduating, coming back to LA and graduating at a private school. I end up going to the National Guards and after I entered the National Guards went to Oklahoma and come back to Los Angeles thinking that the gang scene and all that stuff was behind me and what not. When I got back here, they had a whole new thing. It just became more sophisticated—the gangbanging. The members went from little adolescent rivalries and rebellion to becoming

drug lords. And the drug scene had really kicked up. And I start socializing with some of the old fellas, hanging out. I had a job and everything, I got laid off about maybe, I think, three or four months before I caught this case.

Julius

Julius came to the United States from the Philippines when he was 11 years old. He was met by his father and his stepmother. He had not known she existed. His father, who had told Julius that his mother would be joining them, had married another woman in the United States. Julius and his twin brother did not get along with their father, who beat them with his fists and had them sent to Juvenile Hall. They spoke Tagalog to each other and their Philippine friends and their English was poor. Consequently, they did not fit in with the Anglo and other Asian students who teased them. They began ditching school in the 6th grade and roaming the streets of San Francisco, drinking and fighting with other young Asians:

> "We started gang-banging at 13," Julius said. "We were both bad. We were trying to impress our friends. We didn't take nobody's crap."
>
> Their eldest brother, Albert, said the kids often felt like misfits, teased for their poor English and for speaking Tagalog at home. Julius' education sputtered out after sixth grade.
>
> His first crime was at age 13, followed by a string of bad choices that escalated from truancy to auto theft to armed assault. He initially landed in a San Francisco rehab facility for minors, then at California Youth Authority facilities in Stockton and Sacramento.[18]

Lonnie

Lonnie's father was an itinerant laborer who worked in the fields in the south and then in many different jobs in California. So Lonnie, a black male, grew up all over California:

> My name is Lonnie. I was born in Louisiana, but I've been raised all over California. I came to California at a very young age. We came to Oakland to the Bay Area initially. And then we've been up and down the state. So I've been kind of raised all over California. My father did some of everything. He was what you call a handyman, so he did everything from janitorial services to working in

---

18 Pamela Podger, "A Life Behind Bars," *San Francisco Chronicle*, January 5, 2003.

the fields. So he did a variety of work. He did everything from picking watermelons in the fields to, what you call it, picking cotton the seasonal stuff and all that kind of stuff. He did that, but he also did janitorial services. He also owned his own scrap iron business—picking up scrap iron and selling it. He'd sell it to junkyards and they used to call 'em back in those days. So he did a variety of things.

He dropped out of school in the 10th grade, eventually ending up in Oakland, California, hustling on the streets:

That's as far as I got in terms of public school system and then from there I was kind of in and out of school. I wasn't consistent. I made it to high school. I'm not sure how, but I made it into high school and then around the 10th grade, I just kind of dropped out all together. I was living at that time in Southern California. I lived in a city called San Bernardino and then I came back up to the Bay Area, came back to Oakland, was on my own and was just in the streets, so to speak, from that point on, pretty much. I guess I was 15, 16 years old. Yeah so was like 16, 16 years old, hustling. By that time I got really deep into speed, so I was what you call hustling. We called it hustling back then and so I was doing a little of everything you know, anything in the streets, trying to make a little money. That was selling a little marijuana, doing a little of this a little of that. You know petty crimes here and there. I never got into hard drugs.

I started going to jail early. My first serious offense was when I was about 14. I went to jail for assault with a deadly weapon. I assaulted a guy that had attacked me, my brother, and my brother's girlfriend and I wind up stabbing him with a knife. So, that was my first introduction to what they call the CYA—California Youth Authority. I went to Fred C. Nellis in Southern California. At that time you know they had these places you would go—it was all based on the age bracket. Then just went to YTS [Youth Training School]. I went in there—in and out of jail, you know, in and out of trouble, that kind of thing. By that time I had become involved in the criminal lifestyle, so to speak. I was involved in a lot of criminal activities. And then eventual I come to prison for armed robbery for my first time in prison. I went to Soledad. I came through Chino, went to Tracy, but I end up doing the bulk of my time in Soledad State Prison, North Facility. This was late '72 to 1975, I think. I got there like November, December '72 and I got out of August in 1977. I stayed out two years.

Noel

Noel's parents were Mexican farm laborers who traveled around the west. When he was seven years old, they settled in Stockton, California where Noel and his six brothers went to school:

> I was born in Ohio in 1961. My people were farm laborers. They followed the crops. Actually, they stopped in California, Stockton, in 1968 and I lived there until the commitment offense. I was 18 years old. My people were farm laborers, so we didn't have nothing. But I was a pretty smart kid, too. I picked up things real fast. I got into sports, baseball, every team I got on we moved forward. We won everything. Little League championship and then I got into Babe Ruth. Then I got into marijuana. At that time I was experimenting with drugs and my school record wasn't that great after the 6th grade. When I got to the 7th grade, I started missing classes and I never went to class.

When he was 14, he got involved with other neighborhood Latino youths and together they hung out, partied, drank, and got high on marijuana and PCP. Eventually, they became a gang and came into conflict with other Latino gangs with whom they regularly fought:

> And once I started fighting, that became my lifestyle. Growing up where I grew up, you fight one guy, like any neighborhood, then you gotta fight the next guy. That's the way it was. But after a while, when you win a fight, your reputation grows, each fight your reputation grew and before you knew it, that's what I was doing, fighting all the time. I got kicked out of the 10th grade, high school, didn't make it all the way because of fighting. They kicked me out, into continuation school. In continuation school, you just go from one bad experience to another. Next thing you know you're just surrounded by guys who are just like you. There're getting loaded, fighting. That's where I got involved in gangs. We're fighting everybody and anybody. There weren't even gangs, just other guys. Alcohol, you know. My parents were farm laborers. They were off working. They never got the best of things, because my father and my mother they were just trying to make money to buy food. They didn't have much. They were old fashion, strict, but they were never there. They spoke very little English.

Rachman

Rachman was raised in a rural community in the South by a large extended family. He had a stable childhood and finished high school and was on his way to college. However, he decided to travel to Chicago and join members of his extended family there:

I was born in the South. I was born in Jackson, Mississippi 1952. I had a good family. I had everybody. I had mother, father, grandfather, grandmother, great-grandmother, great-grandfather. My great-grandmother was Shaka and my great-grandfather was African American. He was born into slavery, so I had a chance to meet all these people. So I had a rich, rich, very rich childhood. My grandfather was a Mason. My grandmother was Shaka. I was raised by a bunch of cousins and great-uncles and great-aunts and everything like that. They lived on their own farm, so I was born in the house. My father, he worked for a manufacturing company but he liked to see us back then. My mother was, she worked in the cafeteria school, so I had to go to school. My mother was president of the PTA [Parent–Teacher Association], so I had to go to school every day. So I was at school. My parents did get pride in me going to school, so I had to go to school.

He did well in high school, excelling in math, and his parents wanted him to go on to Jackson State College. However, in 1970 the National Guards shot several students there and this and his desire to do something different swayed him away from continuing in school. He went to Chicago to the fast life instead:

So I didn't go to Jackson State. So I went to Chicago. I got to Chicago. My father's sisters owned their own business in Chicago. It was in the hair care products. One of my uncles was into konk to make hair straight and the base to go on their hair to make their hair straight. So I worked in their store for a little while, but I didn't like it. For some reason it was too structured for me. Today I don't have no regrets, but I kinda wish that I had stayed with that business 'cause I went to the street I went to the west side of Chicago. I seen stuff in Chicago that fascinated me—big cars, fat-ass women, they like you know what I'm saying? So I go on the west side of Chicago, and that's when I was with my other auntie from the other side of my family you know. My father's side of the family was business people, mother's side of the family, street people. And I went to the streets side because I saw that side, that's the side that I wanted to be on. It was more glamorous to me. They was riding in Cadillacs. They had gold jewelry and furs and minks and they was partying all the time. And over on the other side they were listen to Johnny Mathis and had me wearing white shirts and being square all the time. You know, I should have stuck with that side though because that was the best side when you think back. But I don't have no regrets because the fast side made me where I'm at today. Got me where I'm at right now.

I picked the other side over the square, nobody could have pulled anything on me. I'm too late in the game for people to be pulling things over my eyes. Now I can see. I got on my bad side. I got introduced to heroin, not using, but selling. They groomed me to sell like carry me 5 dollar, 6 dollar buttons. Then it went up to 10 dollars. Next it all went up to 15 dollars for heads. Then it went up to 25-dollar bags of pure heroin uncut. Everybody putting quinine on their heroin. I wasn't touching none. I was sellin' just like I got it. You know I make someone nod all day.

But other dealers were threatened by his operation and tried to kill him:

So I got kidnapped. I got shot four times, my face been crushed in on this side. Cut my finger off right there but they sewed it back on. I got four .38 bullets in me right now in my stomach, my back, arm and legs. They kidnapped me yeah, because they were selling the mixed dope and I was sellin' raw dope and all the other guys had them doing scratching and going to sleep. I had 'em nodding. So because I had 'em nodding, these guys kidnapped me and they shot me four times and they broke my jaw with the butt of a shotgun. They cut my finger off because they couldn't take my rings off, so they cut this finger off right here. I got bullets in my stomach right there.

He moved to New Orleans and started dealing there. He was stabbed in the back and he almost died. When he got out of the hospital, he hitchhiked to Los Angeles and began washing expensive cars in Beverly Hills. From that job he went to driving Rolls-Royces for Beverly Hills residents. Then he started dealing cocaine. He got a job for a friend who was hanging around a woman who was "mixed up with" Los Angeles drug dealers:

So a friend of mine came out here too. I got him a job with me too and he meets this girl and I just found this out since I've been locked up. This girl was messin' with some of the biggest dope dealers in Los Angeles, California. And she owed these dope people a lot of money. This is what we're gettin' from my investigators and from my attorney. Somebody killed her and they said that, first they said it was me and him who did it. They arrested me. Matter of fact, he's back in Illinois in jail in crime house. I heard he went back to Mississippi. When I came back out here they arrested me for her murder. And I've been locked up for almost 25 years for this crime that I didn't do and they're just now finding out that I didn't do it. [Rachman was taken back to court in December, 2007 and his conviction was overturned.]

Shahid

Shahid, a black male, was brought up by his mother who worked three jobs to keep the family off welfare. His father was mostly absent and when he was in the house, he was abusive to Shahid, but even more to Shahid's mother:

I was raised in Newark, Jersey. My childhood was one of, I would say, more mental torment than it was physical torment—mental, the way that my father mistreated my mother. He didn't mistreat her physically. It was more mental. I remember her growing up and I remember him vaguely. I can remember him whoopin' us one time. But I remember him more out of the house than I remember in the home. I remember my mother working three different jobs, I think sometimes four. I remember having to go with her. She used to do motel work. We would go from motel to motel with her. There were four of us at the time. It was Roselyn, Vern, myself, and Donnell. I had two other brothers by the same father different mother—Milton and Allen. Yeah, it was toughest to me because you seeing stuff and you're not understanding what it is you see. You see as did I, my father running along with other women and not being home with my mother when we need different things. I remember my mother, the reason why she started working three jobs is because she didn't want to be on welfare. Her goal was to get off welfare, so she began to work three jobs and she got off of welfare. She got off of it, so I've always have the memory of her working. Him, I have to say I don't have a memory of him being in the house, but every so often. But I do remember, you know, when I said that I see stuff but didn't know what's going on.

I saw the way he was mistreating her and that made me as a kid at about nine years old, ten years old say to myself I would never treat my woman the way I see my father treat my mother. And from that point on that became my motivation in life. But at that time, I didn't have a woman in my life. It just something I said to myself. And him, my mother asking us like we have to do hustling. I used to do AM/PMs and what that it is supermarkets and we have Safeway out here, but I would go and I would carry people's groceries to their car or to their house, newspaper, sell bottles, that type of stuff, to hustle, but I was never part of the drug game or the drug life didn't do that kind of stuff.

Shahid's brother, Donnell, stayed away from school, but Shahid continued in school until he was being harassed by one of his teachers who frequently made him stand against the wall while he searched him and questioned him about his brother. So he joined his brother and began skipping school. Eventually he dropped out completely and the two of them "hung out" every day:

> I'm tryin' to stay away from him [the teacher]. And I'm telling people about this and at that time the teacher was right, you know, there was no, I don't know, I just seemed like I couldn't get no help. So as a result of that I started playing hooky, staying away from school, and staying away from him. And then the house burned down from the hot water heater and so we had to move from Avon Avenue and that's when we moved into the projects. And by that time, I had already gotten to the habit of playing hooky from school. So it didn't faze me to move from one school to another because by that time again, him and I started playing hooky together. We would go downtown, hustle, go to the pizza parlor, buy a slice of pizza, go to the park, lay back in the park and then the day's over with and you go home. But we lived with my mother. She's off working, so we had my Aunt Janny, but she was about 67 years old. She passed away when she was 95 years old. So we didn't have to worry about her coming look for us. I still don't know if—I think maybe once in a while the school might have called 'cause I do remember my mother coming in and making us take our clothes off and whoopin' our butts, so she found out some kinda way that we weren't going to school.

After he dropped out of school in the 10th grade, he went into the Job Corps for a year and then returned home:

> I remember I got in trouble one time, I got in trouble at a Nickel's department store. I stole a ring and as a result of that they put me on probation. I was 17 years old and by that time we had left New Jersey. We was living in North Carolina and I went to Job Corps in Kentucky, Job Corps center at 17 and from there, I came back home and from there I end up in prison.

Back home, he ran into an ex-girlfriend at the funeral of members of her family who were killed in an auto accident. They started seeing each other and then flew out to California together. They went to rent a car to drive to San Diego so she could visit some of her relatives.

*   *   *

Four of the seventeen lifers were white males raised in stable working- or middle-class families. Kicked out of school and disgruntled with the prospect of living out a nine-to-five, working-class life, Bryan was "hanging out" with his buddies, smoking marijuana, drinking, listening to music on their stereos, and looking for something exciting to do. P. J. was pursuing a conventional working-class life, but this was inter- rupted when his wife became addicted to speed. Richard was raised in a Sicilian family who ran a ranch and a trucking business in central California. Many of his relatives were involved in crime. He followed their example and started getting arrested when he was 12 years old. The fourth, Rusty, who had considerable trouble socializing, teamed up with "stoners" in his school, and became a heavy user and then a dealer of the new drugs that spread throughout the society in the 1960s and 1970s—marijuana, LSD, and mescaline. Though he had family resources to fall back on, he continued to career around the country getting into many scrapes with the law. His drug use escalated and he started using morphine, methamphetamine, and barbiturates. Finally, he spun completely out of control.

Bryan

Bryan, a white, middle-class male, was born and raised in Newark, a mid-sized, working-class town on the south-east side of the San Francisco Bay. He has two brothers and one sister, all older than he. His father, who was born in Iowa, dropped out of high school and went to work with a company as a laborer, "and he worked for the same com- pany his entire life and he made his way up, eventually becoming a plant manager. Then he helped build plants and became a regional director, safety director."

Bryan had one juvenile arrest for trespassing and vandalism when he was 15. He began cutting school and hanging out with "stoners" when he was 16:

> I developed a love affair with marijuana. I smoked marijuana before a baseball game, before going to school, before going home after school, before waking up, before going to sleep, before my girlfriend, before my family and as a result of that I just fell in love with marijuana and smoked it daily so I wasn't doing much

homework and since I didn't have my homework, I didn't go to class 'cause I didn't want to feel stupid and that introduced me to a culture that was where I'd run into other things like pills. We were drinking a lot and stuff like that. So eventually they chased me around the school all the time I never really got into trouble. I only had a couple violent encounters. One was in 6th grade. I got into a fight over a girl. And one was I think I was a freshman in high school. I thought somebody had stole my sweatshirt and I got into a fight with him but I managed to avoid violent encounters where a lot of people that I was hanging out with at football games or at dances at the school or parties they would end up getting in fights but I always seem to avoid that.

I became acutely aware that I was gonna be working for the rest of my life. My oldest sibling, my sister, was working on an assembly line in Silicon Valley when it was just starting to boom. My next oldest brother was a fry cook at like a Denny's and then my other older brother was working on an assembly line putting together sheet metal parts and so I just didn't see how learning about George Washington and biology and math was gonna have anything to do with my life. All I knew is I was gonna be working for the rest of my life so I decided to have fun and as a result of that, that's where I acquired all the addictive behaviors.

He was kicked out of high school and sent to continuation school. There he fell in with other teenagers who were like him, youth "having affairs" with marijuana:

When I got there it's like wow, these people are all like me, you know. They're having love affairs with marijuana. They're interested in alcohol and the drugs and they're just not interested in school. So I went there and I tried to—I did pretty good trying to catch up with my credits because it was easy for me. I just had to read a couple of paragraphs and answer some multiple-choice questions and I would do good. So I was catching up with my credits and then I turned 18. My birthday's in August before the semester was over, but I didn't graduate. I fell short and so during that summer my older brother got me a job as a labor at a construction site.

So here I am, I'm working as a laborer. You know, my worst nightmare come true, yes. I have to do work for the rest of my life and the common theme for someone who turned 18 at that time in East Bay was to get the stereo, to get the apartment, to get the car, and then you know start to navigate your way through dating and relationships and eventually people who get married. And so, you know, the hot rod car and the stereo where my speakers are just a little bit bigger than yours and turntables were a big thing back then.

P. J.

P. J., a white male, raised by a single mom, grew up in a tough neighborhood in Sacramento, California:

I was born and raised in Sacramento. Pretty poor family. Single parent. Just my mom. We grew up in a pretty rough neighborhood, Oak Park, Sacramento. If you know Sacramento, you know Oak Park. We moved around quite a bit and I was always the new kid on the block, the new kid in school. And one of the very few white ones. A lot of blacks and Latinos. Lot of fighting. A lot of adjusting to the new neighborhood. You know how kids are. I am talking about five years old to early teens. A struggle, but I survived it.

I have one sister. She's doing great. She lives in the Bay Area. We all got along real well. We had a good family life. We were poor and that was a struggle, but as far as us getting along, we've always got along real well.

I got passing grades. I wasn't a whiz kid, but I got acceptable grades. I was always in the principal's office for fighting and skipping class. In the 5th and 6th grade, they put me in Special-Ed. Once I went to high school, I kinda adjusted a little bit. We had moved into a little better neighborhood, and it was a little more stable, that environment. So I did alright, passing grades. I didn't get into a whole lot of fights, so it got a little better. Then I dropped out at the end of the 10th grade. I got a full-time job. I moved out of the house and basically started an adult life, at 17 years old. I started out doing carpentry, then plumbing, then back to carpentry later on in life.

When he was 18, he was frequently going out drinking with his friends and occasionally getting into fights. One night, he got into a fight with some bikers, one of whom shot him with a 12-gage shotgun. P. J. was not seriously hurt, but skin was peeled from his scalp. This served as a wake-up call and he settled and down, married his girlfriend, had two children, paid his taxes, and lived a family-man life:

I didn't even drink as an adult. New Year's Eve and maybe a

couple times a year I drank with a couple of friends. But as far as having a beer after work, I never did any of that. Marijuana was my drug of choice. And no others. I didn't shoot up. I didn't do any of the other drugs, other than acid. I dropped acid a couple of times, just experimental type of stuff. I smoked marijuana from 13 to 27. And then at 27, a couple of months before I committed my crime, I quit cold turkey, mostly because of my son. He was eight years old. He knew. I didn't hide it from him. I was a good role model for him in all other ways. I worked. I was law abiding. I got along well with people. The only bad influence: I smoked marijuana. You know, of course, it is illegal in addition to all the other negative things about smoking marijuana. So I wanted to tighten that up, so I just quit. Other reasons too, but mostly because of my son. I didn't want to be that type of influence on him. I never smoked it again, not even in here.

After they were married for five years, his wife started shooting crank (methamphetamine):

We met early. We met when we were young. She was already smoking marijuana when I met her. The hard drugs, she didn't get on them until about three years before I committed my crime. She got into crank. She was addicted. We talked about it and tried to figure out how we could work through this. I tried to get her to go to rehab and every time we get an appointment set up, she would disappear. I would come home from work early so we could go and she'd be gone to the drug house doing her thing. So I said what about if we just moved out of town and that way you're not around it and people won't be coming and picking you up to take you to the drug house and that kind of thing. And she said ya, and so that's what we did. She quit cold turkey and that lasted about a year and then we moved back to Sacramento because I was a carpenter at the time and I wanted to move next to this giant job that I had bid. So everything seemed fine. It didn't seem to be an issue. And then about a year after that she ended up going back to the same drug house and doing it over again. And that's when it all fell apart again.

Richard

Richard was born and raised in Modesto, California. His folks ran a ranch and a trucking business. His mom was busy running the house and taking care of the books for the trucking business. She had four boys and one girl. Richard was the second from the youngest:

> I had many a whipping when I was a young-un. Started getting into trouble when I was eight years old. I was caught stealing bullets out of a Jensen store. It was just my environment, the area I lived in, the school, what was happening in the school. My cousins they were involved in stealing. I saw them making a lot of money.
>
> I was shooting my brother's .22 and I shot all the bullets. So I clean the gun up and go into town and steal some bullets. I got away with it the first time. Then I go and do it again. I'm walking down the aisle and taking bullets out of the box and sticking down in my pants. I go to walk out of the store and the guy grabbed me and called the police and they take me down to the police station. And my dad came down and picked me up. My dad took me out to the pickup and asked me do I know what I did was wrong and I said, "Yes sir." He asked me if it was going to happen again and I said, "No sir." And it didn't happen again until my dad passed away in 1971 and all of us boys went crazy. My mom trying to take care of all of us boys and we was hard boys. My parents, they were both born in Sicily, my dad in 1914, my mom in 1923. They were more Sicily style. I had family members, they were all involved in criminal activities, pretty deep. I always saw them with a lot of cash. I was about 12 years old. One day I went with my cousin. I was supposed to watch while he takes these air conditioners and puts them on pallets. He tells me to watch for cars that go by and I think he means just cop cars. So I say, "OK" and I let a car go by and he beats me into a mud puddle. I said right there that day that I wasn't gonna let nobody beat me like that and that's what I did. I got tough.
>
> I went from stealing cars, burglary, robberies, collecting money, you name it. I started getting arrested when I was 12 years old. I did two years in the Youth Authority, Preston and youth camp Washington Ridge.

In Preston, he made his debut by winning a fight with an older prisoner who challenged him and then the other prisoners left him alone. In six months, he was transferred to a fire camp where he completed his two-year sentence. When he got out, he got involved with his cousin who was dealing large quantities of marijuana and cocaine:

> I was totally overwhelmed by my criminal lifestyle and I got

involved in a relationship at 15 years old with a woman 13 years my senior and becoming a husband and a father while I was actually still a kid myself. That and many other things had me between the proverbial rock and a hard place.

Rusty

Rusty was raised in a conventional, Catholic family. He characterizes his early life as blessed:

> I was born in a small town called Jamestown, New York. I was the oldest of three children. I was raised in a family. My father had a construction company. His father before him was a hard-working man all his life. And he and my mother got married in the mid-'50s and I was the product, the first-born. I would say that I would have to describe my childhood as a really blessed childhood. I had really good family. My family did the best they could to provide for me. I have a brother and a sister that are both younger and I was raised as a Catholic. I went to Catholic school up until junior high school and my father wanted to have it better for the family, so he ended up building his own home and we moved out of the city.

When they moved to a better house and he transferred to public school, things changed. He had received a blow from a baseball bat that left his face badly scarred. This brought him ridicule from other kids that resulted in his having psychological problems:

> I ended up moving into a school that had a really high prevalence of drug use. And I was going from a real structured environment in a Catholic school to the first time in a public school. It was a lot looser. Let me go back here to give you a little bit more. After years of insight, what I've seen, really, what my problem was growing up. When I was two and a half years old, my father, as I mentioned, had a construction company and the backyard was a lumberyard and a supply-yard and all the kids used to come from the neighborhood and play baseball back there. Well one day, I was two and a half. My mother's hanging clothes in the yard and they were all playing baseball and I was running around. And my cousin, older cousin, was up to bat and he hit me by accident with a baseball bat and I ended up going flying. But it ended up damaging my mouth really bad and my face. And so I ended up having surgery. And I as I was growing, the scar tissue was growing back, so I ended up starting out in school and in my 1st grade, 2nd grade really being

made fun of and really ostracized by the other kids. And I think that they pointed and laughed at and everything and so I really developed a bad inferiority complex. I had really a bad self-worth and self-identity and so I carried this on through school. It got so bad that I used to get photos, class photos, all through grade school. And my parents would pay for 'em and I'd tear 'em up before I, they tell me to bring 'em home and I tear 'em up before I'd even come home and I wouldn't have 'em because I felt so bad about myself, the way I looked and how I was treated. I used to always have to fight all through school. I had to fight because I'd be made fun of so I had a chip on my shoulder and I had a lot of anger issues as a child growing up.

When he was 13, he transferred to a public school where he fell with a crowd of students who were using a lot of drugs—marijuana at first and then LSD and mescaline. He felt he was accepted by this crowd and with them his drug use escalated. He started missing school and at 16, he quit school:

And so I went to work with my father and I worked with him on and off and at 18 I got arrested for LSD possession. That was my first real run-in with the law. And I got, I was facing, this was after the Rockefeller Drug Act in 1975, and I was facing a life sentence. And so my father, being pretty influential at the time, pulled some strings and a friend of his represented me. I ended up getting county jail time and I did a drug treatment center. I went there and I was, you know, using while I was there and everything else. Ended up gettin' out of there and my drug use continued to escalate. I was using methamphetamine. I was using a lot of morphine, all liquid morphine, synthetic. And I was really experimenting with a lot of downers at the time, seconal and phenobarbital, and marijuana and some drinking and so it just kept escalating. So my family, so I ended up leaving. I was traveling. I was living really a nomadic lifestyle between Florida, New York, California.

For the next two years, Rusty careened around the United States, using and dealing marijuana, Quaaludes, and PCB. He was arrested in Florida for grand theft and served a sentence in a Florida road-camp. Then he was in a bad car accident and received serious head injuries. He jumped probation and traveled to California with a girl he met while working for the forestry in Florida. She had a young son who traveled with them. They eventually ended up in Turlock, a small town in central

California, where Rusty's car broke down. They had no money and Rusty was still recovering from his injuries. His girlfriend, Liota, got a job in a restaurant in Turlock and they moved into a motel next to the restaurant. Rusty was using drugs, not working, and taking care of Liota's two-year-old son.

∗   ∗   ∗

Two of the lifers, Vince and Dannenberg, are college educated, middle-class white males who uncharacteristically committed serious crimes—attempted murder and second degree murder. Vince, while in the Marine Corps, was having psychological problems aggravated by drug use. Dannenberg was in protracted conflict with his wife. They had argued and fought. They were moving toward separation and divorce.

Vince

Vince, a white male, was raised in a stable middle-class home. He went to college after high school and then into the Marine Corps where he advanced in rank and got married. Then he started using drugs and spun out of control.

> I was born in 1954 in July and my dad was in the Marine Corps at the time. So we lived in the lower economic class in New York in Brooklyn and then my dad, after getting a job, went off to college. Became college educated and we moved into a more middle-class neighborhood, somewhere about the 8th grade. I was going to school. And then at 18 years old I left to go to school in Georgia. I went to North Georgia College. It's the military college and I went up to Georgia but I didn't finish. And I was under the Marine Corps contract. So I went to the Marine Corps and then 1978 I came out here. I went in actually in 1972 through the basics, but only in the summers and then I had to go in, in 1976 went on active duty. I was stationed at Camp Pendleton.
>
> I was a Marine Corps sergeant. I was a military instructor assigned to nuclear biological chemical defense that's what I taught. And I had met someone in 1978—Ann. We both were 24 years old at the time and she had a daughter and I took on this extra responsibility. Unfortunately I was using drugs and drinking a lot.

As he revealed in his discussions of his awakening and redemption, he was denying the deep psychological problems he was having at the time.

Dannenberg[19]

John Dannenberg was a successful professional. He grew up in Kensington, near Berkeley, California. His parents, both educated with PhDs, fled to the United States from Germany in 1937. John graduated from Los Ceritos High School, in the San Francisco Bay Area, and then in 1963, he graduated from the University of Utah with BSs in engineering and mathematics. He worked for Lockheed and Applied Technology. In 1980, he started his own business—Guaranteed Energy Savings, Inc. He lived a financially successful and rewarding life before his imprisonment:

> I had a normal childhood and adult life with an intact family, unlike most, and I had a college education with degrees in mathematics and engineering. Worked for years in the aerospace industry with classified programs for the military establishment. Eventually went into consulting on business development. And then began my own business in energy conservation business, which was a very successful business at the time, early '80s. I have two wonderful children who are very close. We all are very close. Extended family who helped raise them over the years, didn't have children of their own. Direct natural family, brother, sister-in-law, nephews, nieces, uncles, aunts. They are all behind me, support me emotionally and in every other way. I've maintained by self-studies in engineering and intend to go into my conservation industry upon my release.
>
> As a bachelor, I bought an airplane shortly after I got a job in engineering, a Beach Craft, a Bonanza. Flew that from the Artic Circle down to the jungles in Guatemala. Been to every state and territory of Mexico, down into the Maya civilization, landing on the hard-sand beaches on the west coast of Baja. I used the plane in business, eventually and then bought a twin engine Beach Craft and flew that in business all over the Western United States. I've traveled extensively in Europe, Mexico, and Canada. I was radio ham. I had a first class radio/telephone license. I have a pilot's license with instrument ratings. I have about 3,000 hours' flying time. Basically been in electronics all my life.
>
> Got married when I was 30. One marriage, 15 years, 2 children. They're both college graduates. One has a Master's in fine arts in theater and the other has a Master's in international relations.

---

19 I have used Dannenberg's last name because that is how other convicts refer to him. Because of his pivotal court cases, he is well known as "Dannenberg."

And one grandson and a son-in-law who is a PhD in engineering. Terrific guy. They are all doing well. Everyone is a productive member of society. And I plan to continue in my business in energy conservation as soon as they decide that I am no longer a danger to society.

∗   ∗   ∗

The last two members of the sample are highly unique. Marvin, a white male, was raised by the state. Marvin's father left his young, immigrant mother when he was a young child. She could not care for him or his younger sister and they were turned over to the state and placed in foster care. Marvin went back and forth from foster care and juvenile detention until he was in his late teens. He did not get into any serious trouble, but he was seen as a nuisance by the local police in the small Bay Area town where he was raised. Watani, a black male, was raised by upper-middle-class professionals. He finished high school and entered UCLA. He was radicalized by the Watts Riot in 1965 and joined the militant black power organization—US. US became involved in a bitter dispute with the Black Panther Party over the organization of a black studies department at UCLA. A shootout ensued.

Marvin

Marvin was removed from his single mother's care when he was four years old and became a "ward of the state:"

> My early childhood was marked by foster home placements. I was living in Santa Clara County in San Jose. My mother, as a single parent, had a pretty tough road to hoe and she found herself physically and mentally debilitated and the county came in and removed both my sister and me from her custody and placed us in separate foster homes.
>
> I was four and I was declared out of control of my guardian and placed into foster care. Over the next probably eight years, I was in several dozen foster home situations, one of which, well, most of which, the individuals who had care and custody of myself or my sister had no business having their hands on children in the first place. Years of abusive foster home placements took a tremendous toll. I was in one foster home where the male foster parent, whenever he did not like what it was that you did that made him upset, it didn't have to be much, he would call you over within swinging range and he would literally knock you out. He would hit you upside the head or on your jaw and knock you

out. And this is when I was seven or eight years old. And after about the third time that he did that, I decided that I needed to get out of there. So I really acted out. I grabbed a glass ashtray and threw it through a glass door of his gun case and he ended up calling juvenile authorities and said, "Get this guy out of my house. Do it now!" So I figured out that if I acted out in such manner, that if I was in situation I felt was dangerous to myself, physically or otherwise, I would just act out and get taken out of there.

After years of abuse in foster care, he become incorrigible and was placed in the county's boys' ranch. He kept running away from the ranch and they placed him in Juvenile Hall. When he was 13, they sent him back to live with his mother who had entered into her fourth marriage:

And the guy she's married to when I came home did not want children in the house regardless of how old or young they were. So, I was there about three days and ended up getting into a fight with this guy where he rolled around with me on the floor and was attempting to punch me in the head. He stuck his hand through a plate glass window of the patio door. He was a mover for Levitz Furniture and he had his own truck and they immediately called the police and I went back to Juvenile Hall because I had caused this guy to put his hand through the window. I stayed there about 11 months until I guess he wasn't there anymore and I was released back into my mother's custody. I ended up getting in trouble at school for some other reasons, smoking or something. I got thrown out of school and my probation officer put me back into Juvenile Hall and when I came back out there was another home situation where I really wasn't fitting in because of the person that my mother was hooked up with at the time, again. So, she had me placed back into the boys' ranch because I was out of control with my guardian and I ended up staying there until I was declared a program failure 'cause I refused to speak to anybody for almost 18 months and they put me back into Juvenile Hall. I was placed into a boys' home called Because of Youth, BOY, and I ran away from there. I was taken and placed back into my mother's home.

Watani

Watani, a black male, grew up in Los Angeles—first Watts, then the Westside. His parents were middle-class professionals:

I was born in Houston. I grew up most of my teenage years in Los Angeles. When I was seven years old, we moved from Houston, Texas to LA. The first place we moved was Watts and then from there I lived mostly on the Westside. From the 56th I grew up on 56th, Vermont and Hoover.

My father, George Stiner, earned a PhD in mathematics and taught at local colleges before racial prejudice and alcohol destroyed his career and marriage. In 1955, my mother, Lula Mae Senegal-Stiner, moved her five children to Los Angeles, where she met and married James Brown, a commercial printer.

In 1963, our family moved to a home on West 75th Street off Florence Avenue in South Central Los Angeles. The area was part of a large African-American community, comprised mainly of Blacks who had moved to the West Coast from Louisiana and Texas. Two months before graduating from Manual Arts High School in June 1965, I married my pregnant high school sweetheart, right before the world changed for me and other Black Angelenos.

What changed the world for Los Angeles Black citizens, as well as Black citizens all over the United States, was the Watts Riot. Watani was swept up in the riot activities:

> To many of my peers, the Watts rebellion was a cathartic experience. I remember it primarily as a taste of freedom. At age 17, my participation in the rebellion was enthusiastically random and psychologically satisfying. I felt so liberated, riding and running down the streets screaming at the top of my lungs, "Burn, Baby, Burn!" "Civil War!" "Remember Emmett Till!" In my mind, this was payback for all the TV images of vicious dogs and water-hoses turned loose on Black people in the South. We were showing Southern Negroes just how to deal with these white folks! And the real climax for me was actually witnessing white policemen rolling up their car windows and racing out of our community.

After the riot, Watani, along with members of his family, became more "militant:"

> Yeah, after they had that revolt in 1965, the Watts riot. And after that, the whole community took on a different attitude and became more militant and I joined the US organization and other people joined the Panthers and other organizations at that time. We were really involved in politics. We were in another group.

Sort of a rival group, which is a black nationalist group called US. And there was a shootout on the UCLA campus and they charged my brother and me with a conspiracy. Not necessarily the shooting, but the DA was able to re-dial the conspiracy theory. That's what I'm basically in prison for.

*   *   *

Most of the lifers in this study were headed toward a climatic disaster. Some had lives that began badly in dysfunctional families and only got worse when they hooked up with persons who were living on the edge like themselves. Others clung to a tenuous stability that could not survive the loss of a job or loved one. Even the one solid member of the professional class was mired in a deteriorating marriage. The crimes, like most murders, were generally committed when these men were under the age of 24. They took place in contexts in which powerful peer pressure was operating or strong emotions flared. These men were not cool, calculating killers. They were relatively ordinary, mostly working- or lower-class boys or young men who were traveling on a precarious road on which catastrophe lurked.

3

THEIR CRIMES

Fourteen of the seventeen lifers I interviewed committed murder or attempted murder. (Three appear to be innocent.[20]) Murder is a horrific event that frightens and revolts most people and incites their desire for revenge. However, the public's fear of and vindictiveness toward this crime is largely related to the type of homicides that receive excessive attention in the news media, such as those committed by Richard Allen Davis (the killer of Polly Klaas), the Zodiac Killer, and Richard Ramirez (the "Night Stalker") or the massacre of schoolmates at Columbine or Virginia Tech. The popular ideas regarding homicides and the motives of offenders that have been shaped by the media or "tough on crime" advocates are mistaken or distorted. For example, one usually reads that a homicide that occurred during an armed robbery was "an execution style murder." There certainly have been homicides that appear to be executions, but these are atypical. In my lengthy experience with the phenomenon, I have found that the vast majority of robbery/homicides are the result of robberies gone astray. Most homicides are, though tragic and blameworthy, much more ordinary and understandable. They are "typical" homicides.

Before turning to the actual homicides of my sample, it will be useful to examine the phenomenon in general. We will separate homicides

---

20 Three are probably innocent. Rachman has gone back to court and after serving 22 years his murder charges were dropped. I will describe the details of Marvin's and Watani's convictions later.

into categories with similar causes and then explore some of the social factors that appear to precipitate these violent acts.

HOMICIDE

In a review of the records of prisoners sentenced for homicide, I distinguished three categories of typical homicides: (1) homicides resulting from deviant-group activities, such as "gangbanging" and drug trafficking, (2) homicides resulting from robberies or burglaries gone awry, and (3) homicides related to high pressure, emotional contexts, sequences, or relationships, such as in an ongoing spousal conflict. This breakdown corresponds to national data on homicides, which reveal that, in 2005, of the homicides in which the circumstances were known, 20% were related to drug crimes or gang activities; 23% burglaries or robberies; and 36% arguments among friends and family or love triangles.[21]

Though homicides are *very* serious crimes and are violent and tragic events that take the lives of individuals and deeply harm the family members and friends of victims, most, however, are not committed by monsters or fundamentally evil people. Instead, they are performed by relatively ordinary people who have either been caught up in special, often deviant and criminal group dynamics or in unusual, perhaps ongoing, contexts, such as a hostile and stressful, even threatening, relationship with another or other persons. They fall within the realm of understandable human behavior.

Young people under the age of 24 commit most of the homicides in the first two categories—those related to gang or drug activities and those related to robberies or burglaries. (In 2006, 43% of all persons arrested for homicide were under the age of 24.) A disproportionate number of homicides are committed by inner-city, non-white males. William Julius Wilson describes the high rates of violent crime in the Chicago ghetto:

> In examining the figures on homicide in Chicago, it is important to recognize that the rates vary significantly according to the economic status of the community, with the highest rates of violent crime associated with communities of the underclass. More than half of 1983 murders and aggravated assaults in Chicago occurred in seven of the city's twenty-four police districts, the

21 FBI, Bureau of Justice Statistics, Uniform Crime Reports.

areas with a heavy concentration of low-income black and Latino residents.[22]

In general, non-white males have significantly higher rates of violent crime than white males. In 2005, black males committed 52.2% of all homicides.[23]

SOCIAL SUSPENSION AND ECONOMIC EXCLUSION OF YOUTH

To understand (not justify) the high homicide rate among young people, particularly inner-city, non-white young males, one must recognize the unique and complex problems they confront. In general, young people face great difficulties in passing into adulthood. In the first place, youth in our contemporary society are suspended in social space. They are barred out of adult pursuits—adult careers, sexual activities, and identity and prestige bestowing arrangements. They are expected to wait until they become full adults and then take up adult economic, sexual and many recreational activities. (The primary role of public schools, particularly high school, is to keep young people out of adult affairs for a few years.) In the meantime, they are expected not to cause trouble.

The problem with this arrangement is that during late teenage, they are physically and sexually maturing and acquiring strong needs for adventure, sexual gratification, and respect. So they tend not to wait quietly on the sidelines. They join together and create their own worlds. They party, drink, use drugs, and fornicate—"sex, drugs, and rock and roll."

Lower-class youth, particularly those crowded together in inner cities, are not only suspended, but excluded from the conventional paths through which economic necessities and all conventional gratifications may be acquired. They too join together, that is, they "hang." In fact, they tend to start this hanging early. Because of a variety of factors related to being born and raised in the ghetto, they drop out of school and begin hanging out on "the streets" with other dropouts.

These groups do more than party, drink, use drugs, and have sex. Affluent parents do not subsidize their suspension from adult life. They have to hustle and steal. Also, they get into conflict with similar groups in their own and adjoining neighborhoods that are likewise struggling

---

22 *The Truly Disadvantaged: The Inner City, the Underclass, and Public Policy* (Chicago: University of Chicago Press, 1980), p. 25.
23 FBI, Bureau of Justice Statistics, Uniform Crime Reports.

for economic viability and respect. The groups become gangs. The gangs become tight-knit entities that substitute for families. The members hang together; protect each other from other groups who compete with them for economic rewards, territory, and respect; and carry on criminal activities.

In general, achieving adult viability, not to mention prestige, through economic achievement has become very difficult for most young people. Without family connections or a higher education, obtaining a job that pays a living wage is very difficult. After 1980, the best jobs in the United States available to young people without family support and connections or higher degrees are minimum wage jobs in the service sector—flipping burgers. The income earned in these jobs is not sufficient to enable persons to enter a self-sustaining adult life, much less earn them respect. For inner-city youth and poor people in general the situation is worse. Unless they have family connections, or perform herculean efforts, or have great luck and find a good job, like a union job, they are condemned to struggle to survive in the inner city, dependent upon their families, welfare, or hustling, dealing drugs, and "thugging."

COGNITIVE AND EMOTIONAL IMMATURITY

Moreover, most young people's advancement to adulthood is complicated by their cognitive and emotional immaturity. In the Supreme Court Case of *Roper v. Simmons* (2005), the Court ruled that the death penalty for youths under 18 was unconstitutional because of youths' reduced culpability stemming from their immature social psychology.[24] Barry Feld has summarized the Court's reasoning on adolescents' reduced culpability:

> In summary, *Simmons* relied on intuition—"what every parent knows"—rather than the substantial body of recent developmental characteristics of adolescents that impair their judgment, reduce their culpability, and diminish their criminal responsibility compared with adults. The Court recognized that youths are more impulsive, seek exciting and dangerous experiences, and prefer immediate rewards to delayed gratification. They misperceive and miscalculate risks and discount the likelihood of bad consequences. They succumb to negative peer and adverse environmental influences. All of these normal characteristics

---

24 Frank Zimring makes the point that the reasoning the Supreme Court used in reducing culpability of adolescents in capital cases applies to lesser crimes. *American Youth Violence* (New York and Oxford: Oxford University Press, 1998), p. 84.

increase their likelihood of causing devastating injuries to themselves and to others. Although they are just as capable as adults of causing great harm, their immature judgment and lack of self-control reduces their culpability and warrants less severe punishment.[25]

Feld, in his article on sentencing youth to life without the possibility of parole, examines the research on adolescents' psycho-social development, which is extensive and convincing.[26] In particular, researchers on adolescents and crime have argued that youth's immaturity leads to poorer judgment even though their cognitive abilities approach those of adults;[27] that in "hot" contexts, that is under stressful conditions and when peer pressure is strong, they are less able to make "sound" decisions;[28] that they tend to focus on short-term rather than long-term consequence;[29] that they are more likely to take risks;[30] and that their frontal lobes—the area of the brain in which reasoning, abstract thinking, planning, anticipating consequences, and impulse control takes place—are underdeveloped.[31]

ADOLESCENT CONSCIENCE

"Gangbanging" (engaging in gang activities) and "thugging" (hustling and stealing for money) carry the constant risk of being involved in violent acts, sometimes homicides. All young people engaged in these activities know this and most are prepared for it. However, this does not

---

25 Barry C. Feld, "A Slower Form of Death: Implications of *Roper v. Simmons* for Juveniles Sentenced to Life Without Parole," *Notre Dame Journal of Law, Ethics & Public Policy* (Spring 2008), p. 23.

26 Ibid.

27 See, for example, Frank Zimring, "Penal Proportionality for the Young Offender: Notes on Immaturity, Capacity, and Diminished Responsibility," in Thomas Grisso and Robert G. Schwartz, Eds., *Youth on Trial: A Developmental Perspective on Juvenile Justice* (Chicago: University of Chicago Press, 2000), pp. 271–90.

28 Jay D. Aronson, "Brain Imaging, Culpability and the Juvenile Death Penalty," *Psychology, Public Policy, and Law* 13(2) (May 2007), pp. 115, 119.

29 Elizabeth Cauffman and Laurence Steinberg, "The Cognitive and Affective Influences on Adolescent Decision-making," *Temple Law Review* 68 (1995), pp. 1763–89.

30 Nancy J. Bell and Robert W. Bell, Eds., *Adolescent Risk Taking* (Newbury Park, CA: Sage Publications, 1993).

31 See Sarah Spinks, *Frontline: Inside the Teenage Brain: The Teen Brain Is a Work in Progress*, http://www.pbs/wgbh/pages/frontline/shows/teenagebrain/work/, and Elizabeth R. Sowell, Paul M. Thompson, Kevin D. Tessner, and Arthur W. Toga, "Mapping Continued Brain Growth and Gray Matter Density Reduction in Dorsal Frontal Cortex: Inverse Relationships during Postadolescent Brain Maturation," *The Journal of Neuroscience* 21(22) (November 15, 2001), pp. 8819–29.

mean that they are individuals who by their nature are committed or driven to violent behavior. It means that they have accepted definitions and meanings of the groups of which they are part and the realities of their situation. Gangbanging entails protecting themselves and their fellow members from other gangs and being ready to perform violent acts against their enemies. It is like war games. However, the stakes of the games are real and tragic. Thugging involves burglaries, robberies, car-jackings, all of which can escalate into murderous violence. With rare exceptions, the extreme violence is not intended, but a risk that is taken.

These are not youngsters without morals. Their morals are blunted or twisted. They tend to have strong loyalties to their "homies," or "partners" and adhere closely to the unique, but deviant moral code of their sub-societies. They see people outside their narrow gang or criminal partners as enemies, squares, "assholes," or just others unworthy of consideration.

At first glance, this may see inhumane, mean, or at least extremely insensitive. However, we must recognize that growing up is a process of expanding the circle of others whom one considers to be humans worthy of consideration and that *most* people never expanded this circle to include all human beings. We all start off as completely selfish infants because in our consciousness we are not only the center, but the entirety of the universe. As we mature, the circle of people with whom we are connected and for whom we feel any sympathy or empathy slowly expands. For most people in the world, the circle never grows to include all humanity. It usually only extends to one's fellow citizens, ethnic group, tribe, or race. At any point in history, millions of people are busily engaged in exploiting, killing, or ignoring the dismal plight of other categories of humans whom they believe to be less than human, deserving of ill-treatment, or just non-existent. The examples of this are plentiful: white settlers massacring Native Americans, mobs of Southern whites lynching black people, Nazis exterminating Jews, Hutus murdering Tutsis, Sunnis killing Shiites, Shiites killing Sunnis, and most contemporary Americans ignoring the horrors besetting the majority of the world's population. In view of this systematic and pervasive denial of humanness and consequent ill-treatment of most others by the majority of humans, it seems unrealistic and unfair to expect adolescents and young adults to have empathy for all other people with whom they engage.

In determining our official response to typical homicides, it is important to recognize that most committed gangbangers and thugs mature out of crime. All the research conducted on "careers" of offenders confirms this pattern. This fall-off is more pronounced and sudden in the case of homicide, which, of all felonies, is the crime least likely to be repeated.

THE LIFERS' HOMICIDES

The following are three homicides related to "gangbanging." German, an 18-year-old San Francisco Philippine youth was convicted of second degree murder for the following crime:

> I was with another friend of mine who was in the same gang but I let go of the gang, you know. But I still had friends that was in the gang. And all they say, 'cause didn't want to get involved and all that or more but I still had that, I was still in the drug thing. And so I get on the bus. I pick up my check. We came from his house and I get on the bus and as I get on the bus, I run into the guy, one of the guys on the motorcycle that confronted me. And so I confronted him. We get off the bus to get a transfer to take another bus towards my house. They live like maybe eight blocks away from where we lived. And so we get off to transfer to another bus and I confronted the guy. I said do you remember me? And he said, "No I don't remember you." And I took a Coke can and hit him in the head with it and I told him you'll remember me now. So we started arguing and the bus comes and we get on the bus and we're arguing inside the bus, you know, calling each other. He was threatening my friend that was with me. And he pointed at his head. He said, "Your army against my army." He said, "If you don't kill me today I'm gonna kill you, you and your family." So we get off the bus. I was supposed to get off on a block. My stop was a block away from where he was going. So anyway, we went along with him and got off the same stop that he got off. So we get off, all three of us. And I confronted him. We started to squabble and my friend started talking Filipino and he said, "Get out the way and let me shoot him." I mean, I take my accountability, you know. I'm accountable to whatever happened. So I get out the way. He shoots the guy, you know. [German was released in October 2007 after serving 26 years.]

When Jerry was 19, he was back in his old neighborhood in South Central, Los Angeles. He was out on the streets one day and unwittingly stumbled into conflict with a young stranger.

> So this guy walked up and I assumed he belonged to that

neighborhood 'cause I had been gone since—I left after '79 when Raymond Washington got killed, came back in '82. So I had been back less than a year and get out here with them less. Then I got laid off from this job. So I'm out there hanging with some of the associates and he just walk up and I greet him, thinking he's one of the members of the neighborhood, with the word cuz. Cousin in blood are fighting words between gangs. That's how they identify them self, how we identified our self. And so I still used to use the lingo because this is the community I grew up in, this is the neighborhood. Once I found this guy, he identified himself using the word blood, I tried to deescalate the situation, tell this dude, man I ain't with the gang stuff and I said, I grew up, I'm tripping all that you know, but him being full of drugs and he didn't hear nothing. I thought he had a gun. He attempted to stab me. He pulled a knife out. We were still in the same neighborhood right there we was down on streets—74th and San Pedro. That's another east side of Los Angeles around Freemont High and still a part of this neighborhood I grew up in, though. And so I felt pretty safe there. I didn't think I'd have to be encountering no rivalry or rival gang or anything like that and this dude popped up and one of the younger members of the gang that I belonged to that I socialized with was still active. He had a gun. He started using this gun or whatever he was doing. He stood in the middle of the block, I mean, in the of middle of the thing when me and the dude was arguing. He was trying to make a decision on who to shoot. I'm like man what's going on? And, you know, I had an older brother that was from this gang and he had been killed by one of the gang members, but it was supposed to be an accident. You know, a lot of suspicion was behind it, thinking it was a set-up or something. And so I was still kind of suspicious about that. So when I see this dude, and supposed to be friendly territory, screaming at another, gang lingo. And then this kid who's still active, standing here with a gun. He ain't aiming at nobody. My assumption was, "Oh maybe I'm caught up in something here." So I tried to get away from this cat and I watched this dude, the little kid who was close to me. I end up bumping into him and I take the gun from him. He didn't want to relinquish the gun. "Man give me this." When I take the gun from him, he scats off and this other kid tried to, I guess, he tried to do a rush before I can get at him. He rushed toward me and I turn around and fire. When I fire, I looked at him and he was still standing there. I'm like, we were less than a car length from each other and the little small pistol caliber. So I'm like, damn, I know I couldn't've missed him, that's what I'm thinking. But he still standing up as brazen as he was as when he started, still talking and stuff. But he, and people screaming "Man, he ain't listening to you, he don't shine." 'Cause I'm still telling this dude, "Man, I don't want to kill you dude," right. "Chill with the bullshit and I'm gone." And he say, "I'm gonna shoot you blood," talking this shit. So I held him at gunpoint. I told him, "If you rush me again, I ain't gonna miss your ass again. You better go on about your business." And while I'm holding the gun, the dude turned around. He looked over his shoulder, "Ya, I'll be back. I'll kill you motherfucker, I'll kill you." And I got the crowd screaming you better shoot him. He gonna hit you. I'm like OK, I can't let you leave. I mean, it wasn't enough time to really think. Everything seemed to be moving so fast and the only thing going through my head is hearing this dude what he gonna do when he comes back. I squeezed the trigger again, followed him. He was walking towards the corner. I followed him down, squeezed twice more. He fell. I got on and I'm thinking, well OK, the guy didn't, I hope I didn't kill this dude. I'm hoping this dude got up. When I had time to think about it, but then I ran into the same idiot whose gun I snatched up and he told me the dude dropped, he died. "He fell right around the corner from when you hit him, he dropped." [Jerry has served 26 years and still does not have a parole date.]

Albert had walked away from his group of friends, who came to call themselves the "Little Park Gang." But one day, when he was going to an appointment at the Planned Parenthood Program at the General Hospital in San Francisco with his pregnant girlfriend, he accepted a ride from his old partners. Then after the appointment, he was walking with his girlfriend in the Mission and his former partners offered him a ride back to Daly City where he lived:

We get to 24th and Mission, the bus stop. Wait for the bus. My old partners offered me a ride back to Daly City. Got back in the car. Maria was with me. We forget the bus, I accept the ride so my friends don't think I was a wimp. I did avoid them. I avoided them for a few months. So that day when they offered me a ride, I kept saying no, no, no. Finally I said OK and I got in the car. Maria said no, wait for the bus. I said, get in car, we'll get it over with and go home. Usually we go up Mission Street and get on the freeway and get off in Daly City. This day this guy decides to drive all the way up Mission Street. We get there, Colma, Daly City. I forgot the time, but I would say it was about 4:30 or 5:30. Late afternoon, fog time. It gets foggy there in Colma. One thing led to another. A red light. Another group of youngsters called "the Fog Town Gang" in Colma. They were standing on the corner in front of a 7-Eleven. Like, you know, it was typical, so-called gang lifestyle, you mad dog each other. You look at each other. Then the little hand signals. Then you asked them, "Where you from?" Then the other gang will say, "We're from here." "We're from San Francisco, Mission District," yelling back at them. More hand signals, a few F-yous are thrown in there. Before you know it, the car does a U-turn, drives up into the parking lot and everyone starts running, dispersing. They see a car pull up, doors opening, couple of guys get out. Everyone runs away, except the victim of this crime. He's smoking a joint. He didn't think we were going to get out of the car or that it was going to go this far. Me too, I didn't think so either. He flipped the joint and started running. As he ran, he tripped. So it made it easier for us to catch up. We caught him and the ultimate sadly happened. No guns, just bats.

I go back to that day, I think to myself, if I only hadn't gotten into the car, if I hadn't accepted a ride to the hospital, if I hadn't been drinking or smoking weed that day. I think of them things. [Albert has served 27 years for second degree murder and has no parole date.]

*   *   *

The following are homicides related to robberies or burglaries gone awry. Bobby, who was addicted to cocaine while he was trying to support his kids and girlfriend, went out to commit house burglaries:

And so one night, I left the house and I went to do a burglary. And I found a gun at one of the incidents at one of the places I burglarized and I took it with me and I went to another place to burglarize somewhere else and there was somebody home and we got into it and I shot and killed this person. Soon as I left from his house where I shot the guy at, I walked right into a police who was on foot patrol and he was on foot patrol because of the burglaries that were going on in the neighborhood. And so he happened to be on foot patrol because I'm the one that, you know, stirred up the community and so I walk right into him and he ask a bunch of questions and I end up getting arrested 'cause he found the gun on me 'cause I didn't throw it or anything like that. [Bobby has served 23 years and has no parole date.]

Bryan, 19 years old, went to an Oakland A's game with his best friend, also 19, his 12-year-old brother, and a new 21-year-old neighbor of his best friend.

One day after work, I decided to go see my best friend and see what he was gonna do. It was a Wednesday night and my best friend is pretty much identical to my situation. Non-violent, a burner, a smoker. We'd spend our money on marijuana, alcohol. We would drink it. So he said that his dad and his little brother was gonna go to the A's game, the Oakland A's game, and asked me if I would like to come. You know, Wednesday night, two-dollar tickets. I said yeah and I said I had to go check with my mom and dad because I was still living at home and I had to obey their rules and they were having a close eye on me 'cause I didn't graduate high school and figured out I was smokin' marijuana. So they said yeah. Well it turned out that his father decided not to go to the game and his dad suggested that we invite the new neighbor kid. The new neighbor kid was a guy named John and John's family decided to geographically locate him because he was having trouble in the barrio in San Jose in the South Bay and he was getting caught up in the low rider scene and all that he had been in a gang fight. So they decided to get him out of there. You know how parents if they can't help their children stay out of trouble, they think if they can geographically relocate him they'll change. So we all went to the game.

On leaving the ball park's parking lot they saw two young men holding a sign with Newark written on it, indicating they would like a ride. They picked them up and headed for Newark:

We got the music, the rock music going on. That was another thing that guys, 18, 19 spent their money on, their car stereos, alright. And so about halfway back to our town the older guy, the new neighbor, guy named John, asked the two guys we were giving a ride, "Do you guys want to get some beer?" And one of the guys replied we don't have any money and he took offense to that. He was from a little bit of a harder neighborhood and now looking back I could see he had some cognitive problems. You know we think people that are in prison that are having cognitive distortions. It's a common theme in prison. They take things personally like you said you know what's—and so that was one of them character traits yeah and so right away the atmosphere in the car changed. The music was turned down and there was tension. So I'm in the backseat with the two hitchhikers between me and the little brother who's 12 years old. Now normally with my best friend, I would be sitting in the front seat. But this guy, because of his dominant personality, his age—he's older—he essentially took over that seat from me. There was no verbal or physical confrontation between me and him, but just the structural piece. There he was. So I can tell that they were communicating with each other in the front seat and I knew that most likely this was gonna be a night that we were gonna beat these kids up, let 'em out and beat 'em up. They were good kids. They were college, junior college students. Yeah they didn't deserve this. Completely innocent. And so we took 'em off the exit that they wanted on the freeway and we turned off the first road and it was isolated and we let 'em out and immediately we got into a fight and we beat 'em up and we took their money. But the guy that was with us, John, decided that it wasn't man enough just to drink that beer as fast as we could, you know, smoke that weed as hard as we could, beat these guys up, take their money, he wanted to be a bigger man and he decided to use a knife he had been carrying around all summer. Back then in the Bay Area it wasn't uncommon for the harder kids to be carrying around a bluff knife. It wasn't even illegal at school, matter of fact. And so he decided to stab these two guys and as a result of a stab wound, one of the young men died. The stab wound, he cut the artery that supplied blood to both legs and the young man died. It turned out that he had stabbed them immediately after they had exited the car and I had gotten in a fight with the other guy and so we had chased these two guys they ran naturally and I was going through the pockets of one of the guys and when I turned him over, I saw the stab wound. And it was the width of the knife. And when I saw the stab wound, I ran back to the car and John was chasing the other guy and we beckoned him back to the car and we got in the car and we sped off. And after that we went to a house we frequented with juvenile delinquents. A house that we could just go to any time of the night under age, smoke weed and drink. [Bryan was released from San Quentin in October 2007 after serving 27 years.]

When he was 17, Julius was cruising around, drinking with his buddies and they decided to steal some beer. A robbery murder ensued.

On Jan. 22, 1977, [Julius] Domantay was cruising down San Francisco's avenues with some buddies when he decided to swipe a six-pack from a tiny Judah Street shop. He was on the lam, having escaped from CYA roughly one month earlier. He admits to initiating the robbery, coaxing along the three Filipino gang members.

"We was drinking and we wanted to get some beer. So, the next thing, you know, we decided to rob a store," he said. "It was an instant thing." As store owner Salem "Sam" Totah, 52, reached for his gun, Domantay fired a .22 Magnum at his head.

"I knew if he made the wrong move and he didn't comply with me, I knew what I was going to do. So I'm not going to try and make any excuses." Domantay said. "It was going to either be him or me."[32] [Julius was paroled in March 2008, after serving 31 years.]

Lonnie shot a police officer who walked in on a robbery of a jewelry store he was committing. Lonnie reveals the state of mind he was in while committing the murder:

I killed him. There's no question about that. But I didn't intentionally kill him, I didn't go in there with murder on my mind. I got found guilty for premeditation. I was explaining to them there's no sense in me arguing with you about premeditation or non-premeditation because it doesn't make any difference. I've done the time for premeditated murder, but the reality for me is that in my quest to be true to myself and what the facts are and the truth of the matter is, I did not premeditatedly kill this man. It was a robbery that went astray. Somebody walked in. Unfortunately it was a police officer and he walked in. I wind up shooting him and to this day I don't know how it all happened. It happened. This kind of thing, at least for me, it happened in a haze, you know. One minute he was standing up. I'm saying, you know how it goes, stuff happens too quick, so fast, you're on automation. The next thing I know, the man is shot. He is falling down. That's one of the things that I do know that movie stuff is real about. Stuff happens, at least for me, in slow motion. This thing happened in slow motion. So the whole thing happened in slow motion until he hit the ground and everything went back into fast forward. When you're hyped in this kind of excited, agitated state of committing hese kind of criminal activities, all that plays a part into it, but I think you go into a different state of

---

32 Podger, "A Life Behind Bars."

existence in terms of, you're in a automatic state. You're just doing what you need to do to get through this process and the goal for me was to get the money to get the jewelry, get out of there. It wasn't to kill anybody or hurt anybody, but that's what happened. That's what I try to tell young people all the time, that you can never predict the consequences of the outcome of anything you go into especially with this criminal enterprise, especially if you have a weapon. If you got a weapon something bad can happen at any given time and you can't control it. [Lonnie has served 31 years and has no parole date.]

Noel was out on the streets of Stockton at night with his gang of Mexican teenagers when they decided to rob somebody:

We used to hang out all of the time. One day we were hanging out, drinking. And somebody came up with the idea of robbing somebody. So being the person that I am, when the decision was made to actually do the robbery, who we were gonna rob and where, I stepped up. "Gimme the gun." We chose to go out a rob someone walking down the street. I was 18 years old at the time. We pulled over to the main street, Stockton, main street—Stanislaus—the strip, where prostitutes hang out. So we pulled over there, walked on the street, trying to find someone to rob. We came across two men, elderly men, white. We passed them by one time and we got to the corner and I told my friends these are the guys we're gonna get. So we walked back. They must of, being the place it is, the strip, familiar with the kinda people that hang out there—in my mind they seen something happening because we walked back. They were anticipating something happening because when I went to pull the gun out to rob them, he grabbed for the gun trying to protect himself. When he grabbed the gun, I had the trigger, I pulled the trigger, shot and killed him. We ran. He had $800 still in his pocket. So it wasn't like I trying to shoot him and kill him to rob him. 'Cause I would've went through his pockets. It freaked me out. Which was amazing because living that gang lifestyle, a gang member, an opposite gang member look at you, says something to you disrespectful, you put the jump on them and beat them half to death or even kill them. Then you go to rob somebody, you've never robbed anybody, first time ever. And in your inexperience, not knowing about it, it freaked me out and I ran. But if it was a gang member, if he looked at me, I would've probably beat him half to death. It's just a different situation. Maybe it was because I wouldn't do anything to anyone who did

do anything to me. But that was it. I got arrested shortly there-
after, about a week later. [Noel has served 28 years and has no
parole date.]

Richard went with two other accomplices to collect a debt and they
ended up beating the man half to death:

> I started delivering and collecting money and stuff and if people
> didn't pay, me and my partner would have go and talk to them
> and on the side I was trying to run the trucking business as much
> as I could as a kid, plus I was on drugs, coked out, plus we were
> robbing supermarkets.
>
> And then I caught this beef here with my partner. My partner
> said that that this guy owed him $100,000 and that's what he
> told me, someone I had known through my family. So we went
> to collect the money. The guy said he don't have the money
> because two days before he went and sold the safe to the jewelry
> store down the street. But we didn't know that. So I said OK,
> I'm going to search the place for a safe, so I went downstairs,
> tied him up, and I went downstairs and my crimee is so mad he
> went and slashed the guy's throat, and I don't know this yet and I
> come around the corner to look and he is trying to cut the guy's
> head off. So the only thing I can think of, I brought a hammer
> up there to maybe tap and let him know that it is time to to pay
> up the money, ya know. You owe some money, well it's time to
> pay up the money, ya know. I didn't get to do any of that. So
> what I do is, I know I shouldn't have done it, but I was involved
> in a crime. I know it is serious already. I know that is what
> happens when you are involved in something like that and I
> didn't go there to kill the man, but I went over there and hit
> him in the head with the hammer because I wanted to put him
> out of his misery. I said, man, I'm involved in a crime, man, a
> serious crime now. I told my crimee, "what the hell, man" and
> he just turned his head, you know. It wasn't suppose to go down
> like that. But that's what happens when you are out doing that
> stuff. Things change in a heartbeat, as everybody would know
> who has been involved in any criminal activities. That's what
> happens.
>
> The guy didn't die. He lived. You want to talk about miracles.
> [Richard has served 27 years and has no parole date.]

Upon the beseeching of his girlfriend, Shahid murdered the car
salesman who was showing them a car:

Danielle Blake, who was my codefendant in this crime and we searched around so we could find—looking for a what we considered an out of the way car buying place where we can take a car and—back then it's just a small place. My intention was to get into the car and then drive out and then take the car. But she had been suggesting that we kill the man, too. So I agreed. I said OK. We had been driving around with the car. Well this is what I did. I didn't know how to initiate the crime itself other than gettin' in the car, but I didn't know how I was gonna do the crime. So the car was kinda acting up so I used that as a means to say something's wrong with this car alright so then she started talking—a long story short, he started talking crazy to her. We was playing like we mad because this car's not working you know. I'm driving then. I get out and let her drive, which gives me the excuse to get in the backseat. I get into the backseat with him and she says something to him and he says something in his native tongue and I took it as if he was talking crazy to her, said some curse words to her, which I don't know what he was saying. But I made that my justification as it were. So I'm saying to myself OK, that's the reason and I utilized that and I start fighting in the backseat. But he's much older than me—49 years old. My file said he was 49 years old. I was 20. He didn't look 49. He looked like he was older than that to me, but they said, they had him at 49. And we fought and I knocked him unconscious, but still not knowing how to kill a person. I never done this before in my life, but in my head I'm like, I'm caught up like, oh my god, if I stop it I'm still committing this crime and I found an out of the way gas station and pulled behind the gas station. But before then he's knocked out in the car. I took his belt off of him and I tied his hands up with his own belt. We pulled around a gas station, took him out, put him inside the trunk of the car, he woke and I started hitting him again, so I don't know if this man's dead or alive. So I'm panicking. I hit him again and he goes out, so I decide, I don't know what I can do. Although she wanted me to take him out with some scissors and I couldn't, couldn't bring myself to do that. I'm not sticking this man. I can't do that. So what I do is go to the store, a little market area over there some place. I walk over, get a plastic bag, buy I think some extension cord, I think it was an extension cord, came back and put a bag over head and just tied the cord around his head and he suffocated to death. [Shahid has served 30 years and still has no parole date.]

Vince, a Marine Corps Sergeant, was smoking a lot of PCP and drinking, which he said made him angry and "goofy." He needed money, so he decided to rob a liquor store:

> Makes you kinda goofy, a lot of anger, a lot of irritability. And it was around Christmas, December 22. I don't know if this is what I want and I had a lot of attachments with this relationship and you know we were arguing about money. So that night I picked up a Marine Corps .45 that I had and I walked into a liquor store in Wawona, California and I robbed a store and then I panicked. I didn't know what to do. I moved the guy, put him in a car, drove down the road, got him out of the car. I was really angry, you know, just like I felt like he was challenging me and stuff like that all in my brain but not in reality. And I had him lay down. I figured OK you just stay there you know I want to get away. It's Christmas time. I was to have a good Christmas. I want you to have a good Christmas and I felt movement on the back of my leg and I came across and fired five times and I shot him.

The man did not die, but suffered permanent disabilities. Vince has served 30 years and still has no parole date.

*   *   *

Three of the homicides occurred in situations of great conflict or emotional stress. The conflicts leading up to the murders often build up over a long period, such as those that occur between spouses. Frequently some extraordinary event or chain of events escalates the emotions of the parties involved in the conflicts or sets off a sequence that results in the homicide. Also, in many of these types of homicide, the eventual victim precipitates the sequence, such as in the case of Dannenberg.[33]

Dannenberg was charged with homicide when he was 46 years old. He was an electrical engineer, married with two children. He and his wife had been in severe conflict for several years. Early in the morning of May 5, 1985 the following occurred:

> By May, 1985, Dannenberg and his wife, victim Linda Dannenberg had been undergoing severe domestic difficulties for a number of

---

33 The phenomenon of victim precipitation has been thoroughly studied by criminologists. See Marvin Wolfgang, "Victim Precipitated Criminal Homicide," *The Journal of Criminal Law, Criminology, and Police Science* 48(1) (May–June 1957), pp. 1–11, and Hans Von Hentig, *The Criminal and His Victim* (Hamden, CT: Archon Books, 1967).

years. They had been engaged in marriage counseling and the victim had also sought individual psychiatric assistance.

Apparently the victim was planning a dissolution of marriage and a physical separation although there is no evidence that Dannenberg knew that.

The marriage had been marred by verbal discord and at least one physical altercation (involving the victim and the minor child of [Dannenberg] and the victim) in the past.

On the morning of May 5, 1985, Dannenberg awakened the parties' five-year-old son. He noticed that the child had wet his bed, so he went into the bathroom to draw a bath for the boy. The tub drain was clogged, and the toilet was running. [Dannenberg] obtained tools (a pipe wrench and a screwdriver) from a nearby pantry and in the process chastized the victim for failing to clean the tub properly (apparently he blamed her for the clogged condition of the drain).

The victim followed Dannenberg into the bathroom. Dannenberg states that the victim picked up the screwdriver and came toward him, jabbing the screwdriver at him. Dannenberg had defensive wounds on his body. The victim attacked [Dannenberg], clawing and scratching his left arm with her fingernails, and cutting his arm with the screwdriver. She told Dannenberg that she wanted him dead. Dannenberg picked up the pipe wrench and hit the victim once on the side of the head. The victim kept coming at Dannenberg who hit her a couple more times on the head.

The victim fell down, but kept kicking Dannenberg, who claims that he lost consciousness and that when he came to he found the victim lying motionless on the side of the bathtub, with her head partially under the water of the half-filled tub.

Dannenberg called 911 and reported the incident.

The autopsy revealed that the victim had been hit numerous occasions on the head but that the cause of her death was drowning.[34]

Dannenberg was convicted of second degree murder and has served 22 years. His case is back before the California Appellate Court.

P. J., distraught over losing his wife to a drug dealer, followed them in his car one day and after a brief verbal exchange shot the dealer.

---

34 *In re John E. Dannenberg on Habeas Corpus*, 34 Cal. 4th 1061, 1072–73.

Everything was fine for quite some time and then for whatever reason, she [his wife] got back into doing crank again and this was like the second time of just nightmarish, you know. People who have family members who use that kind of serious drug and shoot it up know what that entails, it's a nightmare to have somebody—because everything for a person doing dope, everything else goes out the window. As we all know, the kids, the husband, the house, everything. So she was going away for a few days doing the drugs, coming back and spending a few days with me and going away. She met this guy that was supplying her with the drugs, that was giving them to her. The reason I know he was giving them to her is because she told me and plus she had like five diamond rings, really nice rings and a lot of other nice stuff. The first time that she started using dope, a couple years prior, all of the nice things she had disappeared because she was buying the dope. This guy was supplying her with the crank and they started having an affair. She told me this. I knew this. It was common knowledge. None of this is an excuse for me ultimately killing this guy. None of that is an excuse I had all kinds of other things I could have dealt with situation non-violently. I could have divorced my wife. I could have moved us away again. I have two boys, they were two and eight years old when I killed this man and when I came to jail and then prison. She was going away for a few days, coming home for a few days and she was doing the dope and she was with this guy. Three days before I shot him, he threatened me with a gun. He had a gun in his pocket. My wife told me he always carried around a gun. He told me if I tried to interfere with him and my wife's relationship that him or one of his boys would take care of me. And this was a scary guy. It wasn't a regular everyday Joe. This was a scary person and he hung around with scary people and so the first and most tragic mistake that I made in this whole situation was on that day when he threatened me, I put my gun in my car instead of calling the cops to say, "Hey this guy threatened me, you know." Instead of getting some counseling with my own issues I had going on, I put a gun in my car. Three days later I see him leaving my house, him and my wife. I start following him. We come to an abrupt stop and I'm right behind him. So I bump the car when we came to the stop, because they hadn't been stopping at the other stop signs. They were just kinda slowing down and then moving. This one they stopped and I was right behind. And so I bumped the back of their car. They pull over. I got out with my gun thinking it was OK Corral time.

I thought this guy had his gun. My wife has told me several occasions, "He always carries a gun. Be careful." I got out with my gun. We had a verbal exchange. I said something to the effect, "That's my wife. I want my wife." And he said, "She's not yours, she's mine!" And that's when I pulled the trigger and I shot him. I had a sawed-off 12-gage. It was legal size, but it was sawed off and I shot him in the chest and he probably died before he hit the ground. It was just absolutely tragic. I mean, there's so many other things that could have happened, you know, but that's what happened and that's what led up to it and that's how it went. [P. J. has served 24 years and still does not have a parole date.]

While baby-sitting the 2½-year-old child of his girlfriend, Rusty, in a frantic state of mind, was trying to toilet train the child and accidentally killed him.

Two and a half then he'll be three in March. This is in December. And so we were potty training him at the time and I kept putting him on that toilet and he's getting off the toilet. Anyway long story short, I shook him, he kept gettin' off. I slapped him a couple of times. And I know now, looking back, I was completely out of control. I had no coping skills. I had some serious anger issues going on. I was already still in pain with really retrograde migraines from the car wreck. Plus Liota had gone out on me and gave me the clap. I was in pain from that clap. She and I were arguing over her infidelity since early in the morning. Every time I had to get up and go in there I was rubbing on my pants and I was in pain from that and all of this was just like continuing to build and build since four in the morning. I ended up shaking him and he hit the back of his head on the back of the toilet tank and he was unconscious and he wouldn't come around and I started freaking out. Her girlfriend came over to tell us she's ready, she's got a break to come on over and I told her run and go get her right now something's happened to John. She ran to her car. She came over there and I told her, "We got to get help, we got to get—" I was crying. I was beside myself. And so, so we both tried to get an ambulance. There's no ambulance service. We bring him outside. We're both running around. I finally flagged down a neighbor. We ended up taking him to the hospital. He had a subdural hematoma and died two days later. Went to the hospital, first I told them (I was lying) he fell down. I told them afterwards, I shook and he hit his head on the back of the toilet.

Rusty served a total of 30 years. A State Court found him suitable for parole in 2007. He was released in December 2008.

∗   ∗   ∗

Most of the conflicts that result in homicide are between persons who know each other. In 2005, 27% of this category of homicide were between spouses or girlfriends/boyfriends; 40% were between acquaintances; 16%, however, were between strangers. Most of the conflicts that escalate between strangers appear to be related to two factors: alcohol and the propensity of males to become belligerent when hostilely confronted by others, particularly other males. The following second degree murder, committed by a 43-year-old man who had an extensive record of alcohol-related crimes, exemplifies both factors:

> I was at this bar drinking with a couple of girls. It is place I hung out at. They wanted me to take them to another bar. I took 'em and wanted to just let them off there but they wanted me to come in. So I went in and was standing behind them having a drink and I felt this guy shoving me from behind. He told me something about my how my son had arrested his aunt. My son's a guard at Safeway. I had never seen this guy before. He was a shaggy, long haired dude and was half drunk. I told him to get out my face and we started to go at it in the bar. The bartender came around and grabbed me and the owner grabbed him and they started pushing us toward the door. As we were going out of the door, I kicked the guy in the leg. Outside, we were standing several feet from each other and he kept saying shit to me, so I went over to him and we started getting it on. I grabbed his head and was holding him. I was stronger than him and he couldn't get loose. He scratched around in his belt where he had a knife in a scabbard. He got the knife out, but cut his hand between his fingers and blood was flying all over. He dropped the knife and then tried to reach it, but I kicked him across the leg and then I got the knife and stuck it in him.

In another homicide involving strangers, the cause is clearly the tendency of males to become belligerent when antagonized:

> Jaime, a 26-year-old Mexican American, who was married with children, working, and had no criminal record, was returning from bowling with a friend. The friend, who was driving, swerved in front of two cars in order to exit the freeway. Abusive denunciations

and threats were shouted out of the windows of the other cars. A person in one of the other cars threw a bottle out of the window at Jaime's car. The other two cars exited the freeway and proceeded to chase Jaime and his companion. They followed Jaime and his friend to Jaime's friend's house. Jaime and friend jumped out of the car and hid behind a fence that surrounded the house. The people that had chased them got out of their cars and continued to threaten and denounce Jamie and his friend. Then the chasers got back into their cars and Jaime picked up a rock and threw it at the car, hitting it. The chasers came back, got out of the car, and the woman who had been driving one of the cars yelled, "I'm gonna go get my .45 and come back and blow your fucking Mexican head off." They got back in their car and left. Jaime's friend jumped in the car and followed them. He told Jaime to get the license plate number. They drove a block away, came back, turned into a driveway, and stopped. They got out of the car. One of them grabbed Jaime, picked him up, and was going to throw him down on the ground when Jaime took a knife he had placed under his belt and began stabbing the other man. Badly wounded, he dropped Jaime, walked away, and got into his car. He went from there to a hospital where he died two hours later.[35] [Jaime was convicted of second degree homicide. He has served 17 years and still has no parole date.]

As the age of these two convicts indicates, many males carry some propensity to become involved in this type of altercation into later years. However, these murders are still rare and unpredictable events and are *not* the type of crimes that threaten the general population or are committed by "evil" persons.

THE INNOCENT

The evidence and the testimony of three of the sample strongly suggest they are innocent of their charges. Rachman, who was involved in criminal activities at the time, was accused by an associate of murdering a woman who was involved with Los Angeles drug dealers. The accuser later recanted in his story and Rachman was granted a new trial. The Los Angeles District Attorney decided to not try him again and he was released.

Watani was at UCLA on the day of a shootout between members of

---

35 Based on an interview by the author with Jaime, San Quentin, June 2007.

the Black Panther Party and US. He was witness to the resultant homicide, but he was not armed and had not participated in the shooting. He was convicted of conspiracy to commit murder on the testimony of members of the Black Panther Party, who were bitter enemies of Watani's organization—US.

Marvin was convicted of a murder of a young woman whose body was left in a marsh area next to the San Francisco Bay at Union City. The only evidence against him was that his car had been seen by a police officer at the general location earlier in the day and his younger sister, who was kept at the house of a prosecutor's investigator for months leading to the trial, testified that Marvin came home with muddy shoes on a day around the day of the murder. (Her memory was not clear and she changed her story several times.) However, a distinct shoe print next to the body was a different size than Marvin's foot and did not match any of his shoes. Also, the District Attorney has written a letter to the BPT that he has great doubts regarding Marvin's conviction.

*   *   *

The 17 individuals in my sample, along with more than 24,000 other prisoners in California, were sentenced to prison for terms of 15 or 25 years to life for first or second degree murder or attempted murder. All of them had served more than 20 years, several more than 30 years, when I interviewed them. At some point during these years, perhaps after a long or short period of just "doing their time," or engaging in the convict public life with its racial hostilities and divisions, gambling, drug use, and gangbanging, they took inventory of their lives. They conclude that there was something fundamentally wrong with them and decided that they wanted to be better persons, atone for their crimes, get out of prison, and live different lives and perhaps "be someone." In the next two chapters, we will examine this transformation.

4

AWAKENING

Awakening begins when lifers fully appreciate that there has been something fundamentally wrong with their former behavior. They realize that *their* actions have brought them to this disastrous end.[36] They come to sincerely regret that they have taken a life of another human being. They further realize that there may be something fundamentally deranged in their personality or character. And they conclude that they better do something about it or they are not going to get out of prison or they will not be able to avoid another disaster if released. They take inventory and ask themselves who they are and what they should do to reform themselves.

Awakening may start early in lifers' incarceration, even before incarceration, or take years (17 years in the case of Julius). Several factors accelerate or delay awakening. The state of the lifer's conscience plays an important part. As suggested in Chapter 3, young persons' consciences are ill-formed and it may take years of maturing in prison before they are able to feel sympathy for strangers and sincerely regret having taken a life. Also, the degree to which persons are immersed in a criminal belief system that condones killing certain classes of people, such as enemy gang members, will influence the time in prison

---

36 Many persons guilty of homicide were not the "shooter," that is, the person who actually took the action that resulted in the death of the victim. These "accomplices" to the crime are usually found guilty of the same charge as the actual perpetrator. In some of these cases, these accomplices do not believe they are guilty of murder.

required to reach the point of awakening. Finally, joining the prison "convict" social worlds—the "yard shit" or the "mix"—with their racial divisions, hostilities, drug use, gambling, fighting, and assassinations will delay awakening. Many younger prisoners are drawn to the prison public life—the mix.

*   *   *

P. J., who was not a youngster and had a developed conscience, started critically examining what he had done immediately after his crime:

> Then I went straight to my mother-in-law's house where my two boys were, my two and eight-year-old boys Phillip and Anthony, and I called 911. I told them I just did a terrible thing and I gave them my address, told them where I was at and then I just went and sat on the couch with my two sons and tried to tell 'em you know, tried to let 'em know that dad's going away for a long time. I did a really terrible thing and I'm going away for a long time. Shortly after that the cops were there and had me lay out in the front lawn and arrested me and took me in.

He continued his critical introspection in the county jail:

> When I first went to the county jail on this crime, I knew at that point I needed to do some figuring out how I got to a point in my life where I killed a person.

Vince, a grown man and a United States Marine who was not drawn into the convict world, had his first insight while he was still at Folsom, a level 4 prison where he began his prison term:

> But then there's the time and I really can't tell you where it takes place. You start really seeing what you know about the problems that you've had all your life, problems that you carried with you. And I remember a guy he was saying, "Oh you know, you ought to read these books. They're about self-help." I thought yeah OK. You know, I got everything I want. I have a wife that's coming to visit. I have two kids. Of course, I'm never serious. I'm always joking, you know, trying to avoid the fact that I'm in prison. I keep them happy, so I'm not really doing a lot of work within myself. Then I come to a point in my life where I walked out and I was thinking all these positive thoughts. Then somebody said something to me and I responded by yelling back at them. And I thought to myself, "Wait a minute. This is the guy that doesn't read any self-help." So you know, then I started thinking about

my relationship with my wife. There's a lot of times that she says something that I kind of like take very defense positions, you know, or get very critical.

Religion has great appeal to lifers. It offers meaning and purpose to their unsatisfying past and present lives, a method of expiation, and perhaps a future life after the one they are living now, which has been damaged and diminished profoundly by imprisonment. Consequently, many lifers' awakening begins with a religious conversion, most often to Christianity or Islam. Also, many minority youth have strong ties to their mothers, grandmothers, and aunts, less often their fathers or grandfathers, who are religious and who attempt to impart religious values to children.

Bobby had had this influence while growing up and his aunt beseeched him to go to church when he was in the county jail waiting to be sentenced. Bobby went to church and the sermon, which spoke directly to him and to his fears, converted him:

So, thinking about how tired I was and I was just burnt out, all the struggling and fighting in here. I just felt tired. I just felt beat down and worn out and so I got on the phone and called my auntie and told her I just got out of the hole and everything. And she was telling you need to do this. I told her I don't need to do nothing. I'm doing just fine. She said, "You need to change." I said, "What do you want me to change?" She asked me to go to church. I told her I didn't want to go to church. I said, "No, I don't need to go to church." She said, "You need to go to church." I said, "No I don't want to go to church." She said, "Just make a promise that you will go to church and I won't mess with you no more about it." I told her I'd go to church when they call it. "I'll go, alright?" And so she left me alone and when I got off the phone and hung it up they called church. And so I had to go to church. So I went to church. And I'm sitting in the back and this guy named Raven was talking about some passage in the bible and I felt like he was talking to me. I felt it real personal you know like a real personal connection. And it's like he was saying things to me like only I knew about my fears and stuff or things that are inside and so I felt compelled to go up and ask him. I said, "Man are you serious? Can this stuff really happen?" He told me, "Yeah," and I said, "Are you sure? 'Cause, you know, I mean like I don't believe, you know." So he said, "Well all you got to do, it's an idea." So I go back to the cell and I was like kinda shocked, maybe in a daze. I didn't know what to say or think. So people ask me, "Man, what's wrong?" I said, "I don't know man, I don't know. Can you leave me alone for a while?" And so from then on my life just changed. And so that happened in '86. That's why I haven't had a write-up since then. I mean, yeah no altercations since then. I got out of the hole in June, I think it was. I never had any more altercations. Maybe I had some verbal ones. I'm still in it, still in it. Right now I'm a part of the usher, overseeing the usher committee that we have in there, part of the service, get their service going.

Noel's parents, who had converted from Catholicism to Apostolic Christianity, had tried to get him to go to church when he was getting into trouble as a teenager:

> They were always trying to get me to go to church, praying for me. When I was in the county jail, my mom got me to read the bible. I was reading five chapters a day. She would ask me to read the bible and I would tell here is what I will read. I read five chapters a day, every day. I didn't know what was going to happen. I didn't know I was going to be converted. It was like a sneak attack. It just happened from reading the bible all the time. I seemed to make a decision. It fell right in place. I did a jail term prior to this murder for something I didn't do. When you run around with a gang and they arrest somebody, you all go down together. Although I wasn't the one that did the shooting I had to take six months' jail term for my crime partner to get three years or else he would have had got seven years. That's when I made the promise to read the bible for my mom.

During the nine months that Noel was in the county jail waiting for the disposition of his case, he accepted Christianity:

> When I got out for that term, 40 days later I picked up this case— murder/attempted robbery. And so Christianity was easy. So during that nine months, I got into religion, and started studying religion. Preoccupied with that all that time. Toward the end of that nine months, I was making this change in my life.
> Like I said, I started on a spiritual journey back in the county jail, so that became my direction, a Christian. You know, everybody has that saying "Hiding behind the bible." But in my life it was real, real experience, because I was tired.

Julius, a small Filipino, who came to prison when he was 18, "cliqued up" with other Asian youth, who were a small minority in prison. For 17 years he was involved in the mix. Then one day, a "homeboy" talked him into attending church held on the lower yard in San Quentin. He was ready for a change. He had matured. He was starting to realize that he had to do something to get out of prison. So he went:

Well with me, changes came when I was 33 years old after at least 17 years in here. 1993, San Quentin, a friend of mine invited me to go to the church. And the church at that time, they were having the church in the lower yard. They had some kinda July 4th service. So I said I don't mind being in the lower yard. You can still smoke a cigarette and have a day and just go kick it with my homeboys. That's what my intention was. And next thing I was down in the lower yard and they got a preacher in there that just started speaking to me as if it was God himself that was talking to me. That's how I felt at that time. It was making sense to me for the first time, I mean ever. I've been in churches, but I never really paid too much attention to what's going on, the people talking, the preacher and whoever is talking. I don't really pay no attention. But this time, it's like I wasn't even trying to pay attention, but for some reason, it just got my attention all of a sudden. It started to pump fear into my heart. I started to fear, this is real. I'm hearing the Word of God and next thing you know I would sit down and something just told me to get up. And I started listening. And it's like it was echoing in my mind saying that you know today and tomorrow is not promised to you. You don't know if you're gonna wake up tomorrow morning and then. So it started echoing inside my head. What if you die right now? Where do you think you go? You can go to hell and that kinda like pumped in my heart and it started the fear in me. So that's when things started to happen to me, on that very day, on July 4, 1993. So I felt that day was a very special day for me because that was the time I felt that God was calling me, you know, and telling me to get right. You better get right or else, you know what I mean? So it's my choice. I wasn't forced to go up there and surrender my life to God, but something drove me on the day that's telling me that right now is the time. You know that was timing for me. So that time on July 4th, 1993, that's when I tried to make things start for me.

Jerry, who came to prison when he was 19, stayed in the middle of the "yard shit" for four or five years:

When I first came in, I was tall, skinny. I was about 6 foot 3½ inches and I weighed about 160. So I was like, you know, I was thin. I had a cold attitude and I would fight at the drop of a hat. I didn't care who you was. I did a whole lot of fighting and I fought a crew after getting into that. I had a manufactured, they called it, stabbing weapon on me, which I carried 'cause I knew they was coming after me, you know. "You got to take orders. You better take orders." So I didn't get to use that knife 'cause they got to me before I can get to them. And I end up going to court, because of the knife I had. Took a deal for an extra 16 months for the knife I had on me with the 36 stitches I got. So that was a good deal. I left Tracy. Went back to Folsom and once I got back to Folsom, I got caught with another remanufactured weapon, 'cause I went back to Folsom with the attitude that whoever sent this dude down here, I'm gonna come up there and holler at them now. And so, I got caught with another weapon. When I got to Folsom, did a lot of fighting and stuff up there, really mostly with my own crew. I didn't really get caught up too much into the racial stuff, aside from that one incident. I was really fighting other guys that thought they had the right to call the shots on me and I felt that I had the right to rebel against any authority. I went back to the hole in Folsom, fighting and all that stuff. And a cat snuck up on me and tried to stick me up there and scratched me by my eye. A gun tower officer broke us up, so we can't stay here. They transferred me to Tehachapi Max. Took the same attitudes I had to Tehachapi Max, fighting and all this.

After four or five years of mixing it up on the yard, Jerry heard a voice inside him:

My mother used to always tell me about praying and this God thing and I know you probably say "Here we go," right? Praying and this God thing and all that. I'm sitting back in that hole and I'm thinking I wasn't scared of nobody man, I really wasn't, you know. They could of brought every person that I ever fought, dumped them on that yard, and I'd go out there to face them. I wasn't scared of nobody. But I sat in that hole and I'm stomping back and forth and I'm angry just like always. I'm stomping back and forth in that cell and I'm thinking to myself, they don't know who the hell they fuckin' with. I ain't no punk. They gonna find out about me as soon as I get out.

And it's just this calm, it wasn't like no real miraculous thing screaming voice or anything, but this calm voice inside me said, "Man, who in the hell are you?" I'm like first I kinda ignore it.

And I just, but I you know I can't say it's a spiritual awakening or whatever. But this voice, like it questioned me, man. It had me questioning myself like, who the hell? I don't know if I was losing my mind or what, but who the hell are you? You did all this shit. You've been stomping through these prisons. You've been acting an ass. You probably left blood and skin and people hating on every line you touched. Who are you? And I couldn't answer the question, you know what I'm sayin'? Well I'm, you know, I had to admit it to myself, everybody got just as much right to their opinion, to their thing, to breathe, and to move on their own as you do. You ain't nobody. You're only what I made you and created you.

Bryan, a young, white middle-class lifer, was threatened by the prison violence and predatory activity. He responded by becoming a "convict:"

I end up in prison and now, I got to fight my way through this food chain, the prison food chain. And immediately I'm getting subjected to sexual predators and what I did was I fought 'em off, literally, fought them off. But as a result of that, I don't know if you want to know too much about that story but as a result of that I took on this whole new identity where I was trying to become a convict. I was participating in the prison culture where we would typically participate in racist behavior being that I was white. Typically, extort from child molesters and rapist and people that needed protection and so I was eager to participate in these things. But it was nothing sophisticated. You're talking about just picking on somebody who's considered weak. But if I could participate with these guys while I do that then I'm moving up the food chain and so that's what I did. And next thing you know, I was subscribing to the convict code.

We had to wear blue Levi's and I said back then the white population was wearing Pendelton shirts and I wore a Pendelton shirt or I wore a convict jacket with the sleeves cut off and I had a bandana going across my forehead and I had my hair in a pony tail and I had the murder-one sunglasses and I had another bandana hanging out my back pocket and I had the camp boots and I had that walk and that talk and that look of a convict and I said when I left my cell every day for breakfast, before I left that cell I put that stuff on and that was make-up because the real me wasn't confronting my peers.

After 12 years of playing the role of convict, Bryan awoke when he witnessed the "shot caller" (convict leader) watching little kids' cartoons on his TV.

I deserve to be in prison for what I did, but I never belonged to prison and I knew that very early on. So I was given the gift where I was always interested to learn. So I took my job seriously and I learned some things. But, I was having moments of clarity where I really needed to really stop what I was doing, smoking the weed and drinking and really hanging out with these guys who are really headed nowhere and if I was ever to get out of prison I was gonna have to make these choices and one of the clearest moments of clarity, where it was really an epiphany, was—there was this shot caller for the white community. He had ordered the murder of a person and these two guys were ordered to go kill somebody over a debt and they went in there and they caught that guy vulnerable on his bunk and they stabbed him several times and they killed him and they locked us down behind it. The whole wolf-pack and it was pretty clear who was the one that ordered the murder. And so it was a couple weeks later. Back then a lockdown like that only last two or three days. They would search the institution for weapons. And in a couple weeks, they asked me to run an errand to the cell house and it wasn't a dangerous errand. It wasn't like weapons or drugs or notes. It was just something to this day I can't remember what it was, but it wasn't dangerous I know that. And when I got to his cell on a Saturday morning— this is a man who is 44 years old, the top of the food chain, has people's lives in his hands, both by who he can have you kill or he can have other people kill you, total control and at the time this is what I was aspiring to be. I wanted respect and on Saturday morning, I don't know 9, 9:30 in the morning, I get to his cell and what do you think he's doing? He's in the cell watching cartoons laughing and giggling and when I grew up as a kid you know I didn't watch many cartoons because I always played baseball on Saturdays starting at nine years old. Yeah, I watched cartoons like the regular kids but not you know I didn't know the characters. And something about that really, really frightened me inside it's like you're gonna make us spaghe ti? Alright OK. I got the roast beef. So it really frightened me because I realized, wow this is really bizarre. So a light went on in my head that said, "If I don't change my life right now I'm gonna die in here." So what I did was slowly make some choices. I decided to stop gambling. I decided to stop smokin' weed. I decided to stop participating and hanging out with people that were considered part of the convict code. And I started to pursue my education and I started to joining these programs and then I started to realize.

Lonnie, a gangster on the outside, continued his belligerent rebelling on the inside:

Yeah, early '70s was a treacherous time. Yeah there was a lot of violence, a lot of racial conflict. A lot of gang stuff going on and I was just, I was young, 26-year-old dude having to figure out his way through it and at the same time I had a chip on my shoulder. I had an attitude about what I thought at that time, what the system had done to me and, and nobody addressing my issues— my anger, my pain and that kind of stuff. So I was quick to anger. I stayed in and out of the hole. I would get locked up for anything, for gettin' into fights. I mostly messed up with the staff. I was always disobeying orders and stuff like that and getting into confrontations with staff. That was mostly stuff I got locked up for. I had some marijuana one time and they tried to take it from me and I refused to let them take it, that kind of stuff. I went to the hole. I wound up going to 4A [segregation unit] for that. That's when I was in Folsom. So when I went to 4A, it was a lot of real serious cats in there and but for one thing I guess for me I was able to negotiate my way through all that stuff and I never got hooked up into any gangs, fortunately for me. I knew all those cats that was in that kind of stuff and associated with a lot of them, but I personally never got into a gang. I just wasn't into that. It wasn't my thing. My thing was, I'm gonna be my own man. I'm a do-my-thing-the-way-I-want-to-do-it. Ain't nobody gonna tell me what to do, how to do it, or when to do it. So I've always been that kind of person—independent. I think that helped and guys, they learn. There was people who challenged me, but they learned to respect and realize that they, what they're not gonna bully me or make me do anything. My mother used to say when I was young, she had this term, "If you kill me you can't eat me," and I took that term to heart. So I've always had this attitude that, you know, hey, if you kill me you can't eat me. So you know do whatever you're gonna do and I'm gonna do what I'm gonna do and that helped me a lot in terms of staying out of a lot of the gang activity and stuff like that. Of course there was the racial dynamics that was going on in the prison. You couldn't avoid that, being the one color, me being black. You know 'cause there was a conflict between blacks and whites and blacks and Mexicans. You had to deal with that. So that's what that was.

Another prisoner stabbed Lonnie and this and a subsequent discussion with his sister made him appraise who he was and who he wanted to be:

Yeah and so I, you know, from that, I went to the hole as a result of that. I got busted, you know. Police ran up there with shotguns and all that stuff. And jacked me up and locked me up. So I went to the hole as a result of that and while I was in the hole, I just started, just reflecting on my life and looking at the things I had done, the kind of person I had been and trying to figure out, what if I would have died as a result of this stabbing, what kind of legacy would I have left? There is Lonnie, dead at the age of 28 or 30, whatever it was. I think I was 30 or something at that time. Dead at 30 over a ten-dollar debt. That was, that would be a sad commentary on my life. I thought about that and so I started thinking how did I get myself into that kind of situation where it came to that and how do I get myself out of those kinds of situations in the future? And that stuff I thought about. I didn't make any fundamental changes as a result of that, but it did begin the process of having me think about things in a different way, thinking about life as if I were taking life a little more serious. 'Cause in the past I just had this kind of devil may care attitude towards life. I was like, "Hey man, I'm just doing me whatever come up, come up. You know, I ain't tripping." And I could always do the time. I don't care whatever they throw at me. I can handle it. In fact, I kind of was one of those guys that relished the underdog position, the oppressed position of being the person they trying to break me kind of thing. And I'm not gonna let them break me. And so whenever I'd go to the hole and stuff, that was kind of like a badge of honor for me. I was like yeah, I've been to the hole, yeah, what? What you all gonna do? What's next kind of thing and that started me thinking about all that kind of mindset that I had that was really counterproductive to me being anything or amounting to anything in life.

And like I said that happened and another thing happened where my sister came to visit me and I was in the hole and they had to visit me through glass. And then I got out of the hole and I was going to the visiting room out here and there was this white guy who was behind the door waiting to come out and I was waiting to go in and he was in the hole, but I was on the mainline at the time. And he said through the door—the door was closed—and he said through the door and I never forget this: "What you looking at, nigger?" And I was like what did he just say to me? And I said, "Man, what you saying?" He said, "You heard me. I say what you looking at, nigger?" And so I was like OK, alright. When they bust this door, I'm gonna bust your," excuse my language, I don't use a cuss word if I'm in the church, but "I'm gonna bust your behind you know what I'm saying. I'm gonna show what I'm looking at." But what happened was there's a gun tower right there and the gunman leaned over. I guess the cop called him. I don't know what happened, but some kind of way he got wind that there might be a conflict brewing and so he came out with the gun and told me to step back. And so they had to pop the lock of the door in the back to get the door open. And so he told me step back and told me if you go towards this guy, I'm gonna shoot you, right? And so I wasn't crazy. I was little crazy, but I wasn't that crazy. And so they brought him out, escorted him. I was like, OK, check his face out and I made up my mind, I'll get you dude. I'm gonna get you, right? And so I went into the visiting room and I was so hot and so angry that I couldn't even enjoy my visit 'cause I was telling my family I got to go. I got to go and they was like what do you got to go for? I'm like I got to go get this peckerwood. Back then I was talking that way. I was saying, "I got to go get this peckerwood, disrespecting me, and calling me a nigger. I'm gonna get him." And they was like how are you gonna get him. You said he was locked up. I said, "I'm gonna get locked up. I'm gonna go do something to get in the hole." I mean this kind of buzz. I was gonna go literally get locked up, get in the hole, so I could get to this guy and try to hurt him, right? They was like man, "You crazy, you got a mental problem." And my sister said something to me 'cause I was like, I used to always tell my family how much I loved them. And my sister said, "You know what? You don't love nobody, Lonnie. You don't even love you." I said, "What do you mean? You know I love you girl. I'd die for you." She said, "That don't mean you love me." She said, "Because here you are you just got out of the hole and now you sitting here telling me I'm coming to visit you and I haven't been able to touch you in months and you're telling me you're gonna go and do something. You're gonna leave this visiting room early after we drove all the way up here to see you so you can go get into some trouble that's gonna go get you back in the hole while we're trying to come visit you." She said, "Man, you don't love us." She said,

"You don't love nobody. You know what I'm saying. You don't even know what love is." And that just hit me like a thunderbolt. I was like, she tripping. But when I went back that night, I laid on my bed and I thought about it. I came to the conclusion she was right. I didn't really know what love was. I didn't know what it meant to love somebody, 'cause I wasn't willing to make no sacrifices. It was all about me doing what I wanted to do when I wanted to do it and how I want to do it. And I was willing to sacrifice myself for whatever it was that I was doing. I didn't recognize I was sacrificing all my family and friends also 'cause they had to pay for my stupidity, for my wrongdoings. And I never took that stuff into account. And so that was the second thing that was very profound in helping me make certain accounts for my change. 'Cause from then I started really thinking about other people and how the stuff I did affected other people, the impact it had and the things I needed to change about me if I was gonna say that I care or love people and wanted people to care about me. So I started trying to make that, it was, you know it wasn't like a flash change, but it was, I was set on that path and from then on I started just doing a lot of different things.

Rusty, after nine years of staying high and just doing his time, began serious introspection:

In all aspects of using, I went years without having sobriety while in the prison. And about the ninth year in, I realized that I did have a chance on getting out again and if I ever wanted one, I would have to change. From that day on, I had addressed every area of my life, physically, spiritually, educationally, vocationally, and every way that I could. And I began serious, serious, intensive introspection and serious work on myself, which I've done for 20 years since.

Shahid started "working on himself" after six years of anger:

I did start working on myself earlier than that but the truth is that when I first came in the prison system that was the last thing on my mind. On my mind was, even though I knew I committed the crime, still society owed me something. Y'all put me in prison for all these years, the government put me in prison for all these years. I can't wait to get out and show you who I am what I'm gonna do to you for locking me up all these years. I was still in that rebellious frame of mind. So no, I didn't think about working on myself until I calmed down and got all the anger and really got myself up over to society or what they did 'cause they only did what they did because of what I done. So but I had to come to that understanding and Transcendental Meditation helped me to realize that society don't owe you nothing, you owe society. You put yourself in the prison, to be in prison all these years. At the time I started beginning to work on myself.

Richard was in the yard mix for 20 plus years, but then his brother inspired him to change:

And they put us in the hole and I'm in the hole with my brother. And I wake up one morning with him yelling at me. He says, "When you gonna quit this, man? You know the game's over, man." He says, "You know I love you. You're a sharp man. You know what time it is about this penitentiary life. You know these fools are gonna rat, but you don't what to live by that old school morality. That went out in the '70s, by the '80s it was gone man. You got more game than I do. But you're stupid. Would you do me a favor and quit this shit? Quit trying to run the child molesters off the yard, or beat them up or whatever you're doing." And you know I was. "And quit trying to walk the middle of the fence. You know, here is what they are going to do to you. They are either gonna send you to Pelican Bay again, but this time you're gonna get indeterminate SHU [segregated housing unit]. You're gonna get it for progressive disciplinary program failure." I don't know they had this on the books. I thought you had to be a gang member, bad, real bad. And that's what's happened. So he says, "Will you make a deal with me? Will you do this? I'll tell you what. I've been doing heroin since 1962. I'll quit right now. I'll make a pact with you, right now, because I know you don't want me doing it anymore. I'll stop this right now." I looked at my brother and I cried and I hugged him. I quit. I walked away from it that day. Shut it off. I don't care. Tell me there's a child molester over there, I don't care. Don't tell me. Do what you got to do. I ain't having it. I'm not gonna tell you what to do. You got to do what you got to do. Get it off my plate. I'm totally through with this idiocy and violent behavior.

PROGRAMMING

Once awakened, the lifers begin transforming themselves by participating in rehabilitative programs. These include educational and vocational training programs offered by the state, but also many programs introduced by outside groups and individuals and, importantly, many created by the lifers themselves.

The programs divide into three categories: vocational training, education, and self-help. The vocational training and most educational programs are planned, funded and administered by the CDCR (California Department of Corrections and Rehabilitation). Over the years, the quality and the range of these programs have varied greatly. Before 1975, while the rehabilitative ideal was still the dominating ideology in penology, there were extensive educational and vocational training programs. In California, for example, during the 1950s, 1960s, and 1970s, basic elementary and high school classes taught by certified instructors in classrooms similar to those in outside public schools existed in all the prisons. During the 1970s, there was a national movement to offer college education in prisons and in many states prisoners attended college classes in prison and received AAs, BAs, and in some instances, MAs. In addition, there were extensive vocational training programs.[37]

This all changed after 1975 when prison systems dropped rehabilitation as their stated objective and funding for rehabilitative programs diminished greatly. At present, California offers basic education and GED classes in which prisoners employ workbooks and instructors are available for assistance. Patten College, a private university in Marin County, upon the strong urging of a group of prisoners in San Quentin, brought a Liberal Arts AA program to San Quentin in 2000. The program is under-funded and is presently kept operating through the intense efforts of a graduate from the University of California, Berkeley, Dr. Jody Lewen. She administers the program and locates volunteers, mostly graduate students from Berkeley, to teach classes.

Vocational training programs still exist, but they tend to be under-funded and often not offered because of lack of an instructor. In a study of the California State Prison at Solano, I made the following observations regarding the vocational training:

> Several conditions greatly weaken the efficacy of these vocational training programs, most important, the lack of funds and resources. Instructors report that they have great difficulty obtaining needed equipment and materials. For example, in the fall of 2001, the office services program had been waiting for months for

---

37 For a description of the prison college programs that existed in the early 1970s see Marjorie Seashore, Steven Haberfeld, John Irwin, and Keith Baker, *College Education in Prison* (New York: Praeger Press, 1976).

updated computer programs. All the instructors interviewed indicated that it was very difficult to keep operating because of the serious lack of resources. The welding shop instructor reported that to effectively teach welding, he had to solicit supplies from private industries. He claimed, "The CDC [California Department of Corrections] doesn't give a damn about the program." Most instructors I interviewed believed that the administration does not support vocational training programs.

[. . .]

Instructors are fired, or they quit and are not replaced. In the Fall of 2001, 11 out of 44 vocational staff positions were vacant.[38]

Prisoners start engaging in "programs" at different stages in the prison career (some of these are described in more detail below). P. J. began while he was still in the county jail waiting to be sentenced and transferred to prison:

Yeah, and that's another thing I found in county that there was no vocations, there was no schooling. They're not really offering anything other than NA and AA and so once I got to Solano, at Mule Creek I did one little program, Breaking Barriers, you might be familiar with, with Gordy Brown. And then in Solano they had a few programs—the Victim Offender reconciliation group. I got into that and a couple of others. That was it from the gate. I was doing vocations. I did shoe repair. I did welding. I did dry cleaning and I finished plumbing last year. And so I've got four vocations and so that was my thing, my plan ever since the county jail was let me go in there and get what I can get out of this place. Let me get a positive program, stay away from the bullshit, keep myself working, keep myself busy in the programs and education. I'm in college as well and let me do all this and stay away from the junk and that's basically what I did. I can't even count how many programs that I've completed. Self-help programs—working with the youth, college, doing community service, working with victims that come in here you know and do processes with them. So that's what I've been doing forever, since '91 when I could actually start doing that stuff where I got to the prison that would offer that. And then of course I got here, you know how San Quentin is. They got everything in the world here and so I keep myself really busy in here.

---

38 Irwin, *The Warehouse Prison*, p. 75.

Bobby started programming by first learning to read:

> I just started making life-changing decisions, you know, like learn-
> ing how to read. It was fast. That's what shocked me, how fast I
> was learning but then I guess within three years I was on my own,
> really. Basically, I was doing well. In three years, I took the test and
> I didn't pass it. I missed by, I think, I missed it by six points or
> something like that. I missed it by six. That was 9th grade equiva-
> lency. I'm above that. I'm at a 10th grade, 10 point perform at a
> 10th grade level of reading, which is good. I never took the college
> here, though. I still struggle with some kind of reading problem,
> not bad just I do have one though. I'm not a fast reader but I can
> read though. I use a dictionary sometimes. I most definitely can
> read now. I can read. It's never a problem writing. I can always
> write but you can't read. If you can't read you can't write. No, I
> disagree. I can write. I just can't read. I took a whole bunch of
> programs. Let me see. What are all the programs? I took the Non-
> Violent Project program because the board told me I need to take
> up some non-violent programs. I took, let me see, Non-Violent
> Communication, I took up, well I'm still in IMPACT. I've been in
> the IMPACT two modules now, so I attend that one. I went to
> VORG, which is Victim Awareness Group, still involved in that.
> I'm in the Next Step. I'm also in the drug and alcohol program in
> the chapel over there where I'm training to be a counselor, still
> going to school for that. What else? Got all the—I went through
> three or four vocational trades. I took all the vocational trades. I
> took one in Lancaster and two through here and right now I'm in
> one that's closed down, landscaping. I just got into that one for
> the fun of it. I'm doing pretty well. I'm still active in all the
> groups. I'm not in SQUIRES or anything like that, but I tried to
> stay bound in other groups.

German began his "programming" after serving six years:

> Yeah, right there in '85 you know I figured I better change my life
> if I ever want to get out of prison and so I start going to school. I
> took a trade and stuff. But I was going to school even when I first
> came to prison in San Quentin. Got my high school diploma. I
> started here in San Quentin, started going to high school and
> went to Tracy. That's where I completed the high school, took a
> couple of grades and then later on in '89, I started taking college
> courses, taking a theology class. I'm taking regular college from
> Delta College and then in '91 I was sent to San Quentin for a

Category X psychological evaluation. There was a three-month program. I ended up staying here and so I was endorsed to San Quentin after finished the Cat. X and I started going to school here. When I first got here there wasn't too many programs and as the years went by there's a lot of volunteers begin to do programs, begin to do TRUST, begin to do IMPACT and open all these programs and so I got involved in all that. I got involved with the Patten College. They brought Patten College here so you can get your AA. I think it was '95, somewhere there, early '90s in the middle '90s, they brought the Patten College. So a guy that goes to Patten can get his AA. I have my AA. I graduated and got my degree in AA, liberal arts. Also got a certificate, ministry certificate from Patten College and I also I am involved now with a substance abuse where they certified us to be counselors substance abuse counselor with Cat. X.

Jerry made a promise to remake himself and began programming:

I did everything I said. I made an another promise: I'm gonna make myself, I'm gonna improve in every area in my life, in physical, mental, spiritual and that's what I did. I get two trades. I finished one trade right before I left Tehachapi in '89. Did another one in Wasco, years later. I mean, that's pretty much my whole thing is on that and that's what I try to do now. I try to reach out. I try to teach other dudes the same thing, man. And all you got to do is be in control of you. You cannot be responsible about what some other fool gonna do man. If you do, you're gonna drive yourself crazy, like I practically would of did to myself. All you got to do is control yourself, your own actions, be responsible for yourself.

Went back and got my GED. Started a spiritual program. I started programming in Calipat' [Calipatria State Prison], my first Associate degree in religious theology and kept on that. Did my three years there. Come to San Quentin in 2001. Landed here and finished that Associate degree in 2001. Started my second Associate degree in general education here. Finished that, you know, that's pretty much what I've been doing.

Rusty followed his introspection with extended programming:

I've got two college degrees right now, an AA degree, liberal arts from Chapman and I ended up finishing it here with Patten. When I came to this institution, they had no opportunities here at all. And I met with an old administrator and brought in a college program here. We were gonna originally get Cal State Hayward and we ended up bringing in Patten. I was instrumental in that, in bringing that college program to San Quentin. And I got my liberal arts degree here, was the first one to graduate since they brought the college program back. Then I continued. I carried that on myself with my family and I ended up getting a Bachelor's degree with University California, Coast University, three years later. I've got two vocational trades. I became quite skilled at sheet metal and some welding. I also have performed work as a clerk in almost every capacity in every position within a facility.

I've currently certified by the State of California as rape crisis counselor. I've also had 85 hours as a crisis intervention counselor. Another fellow, good friend of mine in here that I've known for years, we co-founded a group called Brothers Keepers, which is a group that really began as a suicide prevention group and it continued to expand into all areas of crisis intervention. And I've completed that with a certification in that. I'm currently what they call a CADCA (California Alcohol and Drug Counselor Associate) registered alcohol and drug intern with the State of California. And I'm in my active internship now since I finished the practicum. I finished the classes necessary after 22 months in November and the practicum and now I'm accumulating intern hours. And June 8, I will take the first phase of testing for certification in California. It's never been done before and I was instrumental with one other inmate in bringing that program to CDC [California Department of Corrections], which is the first program of its kind probably in the United States, definitely in California. And there's 11 of us now that are actually going be registered drug and alcohol counselors. We developed drug and alcohol program with clinicians from the street that's comparable to any drug program you would find in the street. Our practicum clinician is the current director of Mt. Diablo Medical Pavilion here in Walnut Creek and the other clinician, who is our program clinician for the programming here as Full Circle Recovery Services. She was a 20-year clinician at Kaiser Hospital. And those two along with the rest of us developed this drug treatment center modeled as the same way Mt. Diablo and Kaiser would be on the street. We brought it into the facility and on Fridays, we conduct a drug treatment center here for the course of the day while we're accumulating our intern hours. And so we are actively getting our philosophy, which is a seamless continuum of care that begins within the facility that these men go through, 16 weeks of extensive psycho-education and one-on-one case management with interns and process groups they will finish 48 classes in the course of 16 weeks to get them started in a life of recovery. Many of which have been multiple offenders and never had this opportunity before or had the opportunity and never been able to fulfill a life of recovery and a changed life. And now we're offering this opportunity for the first time in the Department of Corrections in this intensity with guys that are going through adversities that they are within a prison setting. And so far, we've got nothing but guys that have done programs in the system for 25 years, have never done a program that's given them what this program has. The reports, I mean they, any of them, can be interviewed. They can tell the extent and the impact that this program has had on their lives so.

As the quotes from prisoner interviews reveal, there are numerous self-help programs at San Quentin, most of which were created by prisoners. The process for creating a program may start with a group of prisoners with an interest in some form of self-help activities. They plan a program and write a proposal to the warden for approval. The program must have a sponsor who may be a prison staff member or an approved outsider. Some of the programs were introduced to the prison by staff or outsiders who have an interest in some self-help activity and become sponsors of the programs. Because San Quentin, during the 1990s and 2000s, had several liberal wardens who supported rehabilitative activities and because it is located in the San Francisco Bay Area, close to San Francisco itself, where a large number of socially active citizens reside, it has more self-help programs than any of the other 31 California state prisons. The following are a few of these programs at San Quentin:

ARC (Addiction Recovery Counseling)
A 16-week drug and alcohol addiction program offered by professionally trained peer inmate counselors. The program includes psycho-education classes in the areas of understanding addiction, relapse, prevention and life skills.

IMPACT (Incarcerated Men Putting Away Childish Things)
This program was created by a group of prisoners in cooperation with the Protestant Chaplain. The stated purpose is to "reform the character of men seeking to bring their lives to full and responsible maturity."

Katargeo Rehabilitation Program

Katargeo is San Quentin's longest running rehabilitation program. The name refers to freeing yourself from that which binds you. According to the program, everybody gets a hand of cards in life. Some are good, some are bad cards, and nobody gets to do the shuffling. Most of us try to change the cards; we try to control the circumstances we are in, and discover (often too late) how frustrating that is. In this class the focus shifts from circumstances to developing individuals' stance in life: How to embrace their fate and find their power by learning how to deal with what's in front of them.

Keeping it Real

Keeping it Real is a life skills/peer education course designed, developed, and facilitated by inmates. It brings a unique focus to many of the issues seen as important to the inmate population, such as "removing the mask(s)," "self-validation," "building positive relationships," "healing the wounded father and son relationships," "role models for success," "fear of success/fear of failure," "racism and prejudice," "from a woman's perspective," and "getting the prison out of us," all within the concept of keeping it real with self and others.

Manalive

The Manalive class provides a supportive environment in which men explore how they came to adopt a belief system (known as the Male-Role Belief System) in which they expect to have authority over and services from their partners. The class studies how this belief system has led them to violent behavior. The program teaches that men use physical, verbal, emotional and sexual violence to enforce their superiority over their partners.

NVC (BASIC) (Non-Violent Communication—Basic)

Through discussions, role-plays, and practicing exercises carried on in 12 consecutive classes, participants learn tools for preventing conflict, resolving conflict, creating better relationships, really listening, meeting needs peacefully, transforming anger, cooperative learning, team building and bridging cultural differences.

NVC (NEXT STEP) (Non-Violent Communication—Next Step)

Next Step offers more in-depth training and practice than NVC—BASIC.

No More Tears
> Another program created by prisoners at San Quentin with the purpose of inducing individuals to take responsibility for their actions.

San Quentin TRUST
> TRUST is a program brought to San Quentin by Dr. Gary Mendez who started a similar program in New York. Its purpose is to teach prisoners responsibility utilizing sociological training. It engages prisoners in weekly "workshops" focused on such topics as "purging," "identifying," "history and culture." A sociology professor from University of San Francisco leads the workshops and many student volunteers from USF participate.

Project Reach
> Project Reach pairs literate prisoners with those striving to learn. This program was created by prisoners.

Brothers Keepers
> A peer support group that provides crisis intervention and suicide prevention services to San Quentin's population. It was started by two prisoners after one of their friends committed suicide.

Several groups bring prisoners and outside youth or victims together for counseling, reconciliation, and restorative justice efforts.

SQUIRES (San Quentin Utilization of Inmate Resources, Experience, and Studies)
> Started in 1964, SQUIRES brings California Juvenile wards and probationers to San Quentin for "intervention," which is undertaken by San Quentin prisoners.

REAL Choices
> Two prisoners and San Quentin Lieutenant Crittendon started this youth intervention program in 2001. Young people from around the Bay Area come to San Quentin for counseling from lifers who, employing their experience and their transformation, try to guide the youth to more responsible and productive lives.

VORG (Victim Offender Reconciliation Group)
> Initiated by the Bay Area's Women Against Rape organization, VORG brings rape victims together with prisoners for reconciliation efforts.

*   *   *

The final stage in lifers' transformation is their involvement in these intense, organized activities that are aimed at, first, making fundamental changes in the prisoners' orientations to life, and then to offer services to outsiders. It must be emphasized that these are not programs planned and administered by the CDCR, though they must be approved by the administration. These "self-help" activities have been either created by the lifers themselves or by lifers in cooperation with volunteers, most of them "outsiders," and have been sustained by the commitment and participation of the lifers. Consequently, they avoid the problems that greatly weakened rehabilitative programs introduced and administered by the prison system. Mainly, prisoners willingly participate in them and they do not tailor their participation with the intention of receiving favorable evaluations from the prison staff functionaries who supervised the programs.[39]

I must note that all these programs focus on correcting deficiencies in the individual, e.g. his violent tendencies, poor cognition, need for anger management, denial of shortcomings, deficient education, or lack of vocational skills. Programs that analyze social stratification, minority status, racial prejudice, or other social factors that impinge on individuals and may have been instrumental in their criminal history are not approved. For example, there are no African-American or Chicano history programs and no Marxist or socialist study groups.[40]

---

39 See Irwin, *Prisons in Turmoil*, pp. 44–45, for a discussion of the corruption of treatment programs during the rehabilitative era.

40 In the 1960s and 1970s, these more "radical" approaches to transformation began appearing in prisons across the country. However, after a decade of turmoil, prison administrators systematically suppress them. See ibid., Chapter 5.

5

ATONEMENT

The 14 guilty lifers interviewed for this study have expressed extreme remorse for their crimes and have gone to great lengths to atone for the harm they caused others, particularly the families of the victims of their crimes. This atonement passed through several stages. It started with the awakening discussed in the preceding chapter. Then it passed through a painful process of accepting full responsibility for their crime. Then, usually through the participation in some of the programs described in the previous chapter, it involved gaining insights into their faults and shortcomings, e.g. their self-centeredness, selfishness, irresponsibility, and immaturity. This was followed by their attempts to acquire a responsible and socially beneficent orientation. Finally it has ended with their making plans for living out this orientation when they are released.

SELF-INVENTORY

Bobby, after turning to religion in the county jail, went astray, but came back to Christianity to resolve his guilt and shame:

> When I got to Folsom prison and I wasn't going with the script that I was confessing to go with. There were a few guys who I knew, I didn't know, but they knew of me. I was associating with them and they heard me talk and I wasn't talking like I was a changed person. And they said, "Heh, man, I thought you was a Christian?" I said, "I am." They said, "Well, they don't act like

that." So from that point on I tried to make a change internal, like inside, because all that I was doing was all up in my head. I was making changes there. I took a spiritual journey to make those changes, like the person, the smoking, all that in myself that I was holding on to that was preventing me from having a relationship. Because I changed without the system, with nobody pushing me to change. I made the decision to change because of the shame and guilt associated with the crime I committed. So as long as I was acting out, I was keeping the crime buried down. Once I started dealing with the things that were holding me back, then I started dealing with the shame and guilt.

Bryan was somewhat reluctantly involved in the attack on the two young hitchhikers whom he and his companions picked up and then proceeded to accost and rob. He did not perform the actual knifing of the young man who died. After several years of denial, he finally confronted and accepted his responsibility in the murder:

I still rationalized and mitigated things, I still got—because I wasn't the actual perpetrator, the wielder of the knife, that I was different. You know one of things I learned is that one of the hardest things for me to reconcile with is that I saw that person there with that stab wound. I saw that and I ran and I left him there and he bled to death. So no matter what my codependency, I left another human being there to die and it really, really takes a sick individual to do that. And one of the things that I learned you know 'cause I've really had to understand how did I come to a point in my life where I was able to do that. You could say that I had been drinking. You could say that I wasn't responsible 'cause I didn't—'cause I did get scared and I did run. I remember as a child when I was acting out, getting into trouble, parents and the school teachers, my counselors they would always say, you know it seems like you don't care about nobody except yourself. Can't you see what you're doing to this family? Can't you see what you're doing to this school? You don't care about no one but yourself, so I believed that. And so for years I thought that I participated in that crime and I was able to leave that person there to bleed to death because I didn't care about anybody except myself. But the truth is that it was only because I did not care about myself that I was able to leave that person. I couldn't care about that person there on the ground because I didn't care about myself.

German, though he was not the "shooter" in his crime, finally took full responsibility for the murder:

> I mean even though I'm not the shooter but, you know, I take full responsibility for this man's life and I take ownership of what I did. I'm as guilty as the shooter and I'm responsible for it. And I'm not trying to deny I'm not bitter about my situation when I've got 28 years and I'm not the shooter. But I'm as guilty as the shooter and you know they ask me at the board about my crime partner. How I feel I have to be able to count for myself today, you know, being out to give an account somewhere down the line whether it be—that's my belief my faith is that he has to give an account someday somewhere. But me, I'm giving an account today for what I've done.
>
> I was there I was involved I was in it you know and I'm not trying to deny, I'm not trying to play all this I'm innocent stuff. I'm not innocent, you know. I'm as guilty as the shooter and I accept that responsibility. People need to understand that you know like they think I'm trying to minimize my role. I'm not trying to minimize. I was there. I could have stopped him from shooting this man. I could have said, no don't shoot him. You know I had that authority to tell him that but I didn't do that. I cooperated with him. Then when he was shot. I didn't try to call no ambulance. I didn't try to save the man, so I'm accountable for that. Although at the beginning of my sentence I was bitter towards him. I was mad. But I come to realize what I have to be able to account for myself and this is me now. This is when I transformed my life. I realized I have to give an account for myself and nobody else. And I feel good about it you know. I don't feel bitter towards my crime partner or whether he's on the street doing good or whatever today. I'm taking care of me. I have to take care of me and I'm doing this time. You know, it may seem to other people it's unfair, but it's, to me, it's fair 'cause we all got to give an account somewhere somehow down the line however it is whatever they call karma or however they call it but I believe that we have to account for every, every action that we make.

Julius' religion led him to recognize that he was acting like a selfish child:

> You know let me try this other side there's got to be more to it, to life, than just being this and being that. You know now finally there's hope. I was introduced to hope and to me that's what Jesus

Christ, he introduced me to that, you know. There's more to it and he started revealing not only himself to me but he started revealing myself to me. He started showing me what I was really born for, why I was on his planet for. And he's really not really just all about Jesus. It's not just about that. It's about God first and then it's about me and my family and then it's about my community. That's what to me, what life is really all about. But all this time I was being selfish. I was being foolish. I was acting like a child. Even the bible says that. You know when I was a child, I thought like a child, I acted like a child. But when I became a man, I put all foolishness and all childish ways behind. So this was introduced to me.

Lonnie recognized that the crime he committed was a "tragedy beyond repair" to the victim and his family:

I'm a 56-year-old man and I'm a mature adult now and I have complete control of my faculties now. I've had the chance to look at myself, look at my life, analyze my mistakes, the good parts of my life along with the bad parts of my life, the things that drove me to the kind of actions I took that led me to crime in the first place, the things that led me to this crime. I looked at all those things that I've come to a lot of understanding about.

What I did was a human tragedy. The crime I committed against the Willis family and Mr. Willis was a human tragedy beyond repair.

While in jail waiting for trial, Noel threw himself into religion and this precipitated his self-inspection:

I became a Christian because I needed help at the time, 18 years old. My crime partners had turned on me. Facing the death penalty. Jail house religion, the way to grab someone's attention. A way to get into, tell them that God can get them out. They don't tell them that it may not happen right away. If it does happen, you have to be honest with yourself and with the people that you hurt before you can be right with God. That's the sticking point right there, that's where it shows if you have changed or want to change. It doesn't always work out like that. That's what they told me. God would get me out. And so I threw myself into it. What it did was show me what I was, who I was. Eighteen and I was already charged with three murders. Already been in jail for violence, gang activities. Showed me how short is life. Not a pretty picture, but it had a profound effect upon me, because it provoked me to change to the point where I pled guilty to my crimes, because I wanted to start anew. Could I have received the same amount of time had I not committed my life to Christ? Probably. Had I went to trial and not given my life to God? But at that point that what was happening to me.

It gave me insight into who I was, what I was doing. It gives you a framework to work on issues. It is like the light being out in a house and the light goes on, you see the house is disorganized. Who did that? But it's your own house. It's you. As time went on, once I came to prison, the programs that were in the prison helped me to sort out my house, gave me the answers to the questions, provided ways to straighten out. If you don't know them. You have to change your mindset. My mindset was warped. That's what I had to see. This culture I had gotten into, street life, the code of the streets, some people call it. Mexicans call it La Vida Loca. My belief system was shot.

P. J. needed appropriate programs to assist him in figuring himself out:

I needed to find my way through the system and find resources that I could get at to where I could figure myself out. So, except for earning my high school diploma in a tutoring program while I was in the county jail, that really didn't happen until about five years into my prison time to when I actually got to a prison, San Quentin, where they offered programs—anger management and psychological type programs, group counseling, therapy, things like that to where I could really start delving into what internally was going on with me to get to the point that I got in my life of being in prison for murder. That started here in the early '90s. It was a gradual process as far as doing positive things. It started out with my education. I got my high school diploma in the county jail. And then I pursued college. Then college got shut down because they took the state funding for that. And then there were some lightweight programs in the other prisons I was at. One was Breaking Barriers with Gordon Graham talking about positive self-talk and setting goals—to set small goals to get to bigger goals. So I sort of started gradually. I don't think there was a major turning point or major event that happened in prison that caused me to say, "Oh man, I gotta figure this out," because I had already started that process soon after I shot Charley. I started figuring it out then. That was a terrible event to get to to have to figure it out, but I was at a point then to where my responsibilities were exploded up to much more than they were before that point—paying the bills, working, taking care of my family. Not to mention my own emotional junk that I'd been stuffing for all my life and then the situation of my wife leaving me to go back to using drugs and her having an affair with her drug dealer. It was all more than I was capable of handling at the time. It became my responsibility of figuring myself out and growing up.

Before he died in prison, Richard's brother inspired Richard to "wake up:"

God sent my brother to me because he knew my brother was gonna die. He knew my brother was gonna die and he knew they weren't gonna let him come and visit me because of all the drugs he had been involved in. He sent him to get me the message to wake me up out of my sleep and help me to understand, to stop acting like a stupid moron and start waking up because this life here has all been a façade, living like an animal, living contrary to the normal way of life: working hard, paying bills, being accountable, being responsible, and being intimate with those people you interact with.

Rusty, who had used drugs from an early age until he was arrested for the current homicide, continued to use drugs in prison for the first nine years. Then he began working on himself.

For the first nine years in prison, I was caught up in the self-deception of addiction. And I was caught up in the selfishness. The self-centered attributes of addiction were still playing themselves out after I came to prison. For me, I think what initially what it was was the threat of not getting out again, of having to go to the board. Because of that, that was enough incentive for me to go ahead, to take another look. I had had enough tragedy in my life—car wreck, having my best friend die, and then the tragedy of this case, coming to prison because of this. And still I didn't get it. It wasn't enough for me. Coming here, doing a life sentence, now. Aging and I am getting to a level of maturity and then starting to go ahead. You know what, this isn't working anymore. I had an epiphany on the yard. I saw an old guy walking across the yard with a cane and it was like God telling me that that is going to be you if you don't change. It was like a transforming moment like what they talk about in 12 steps. A level of consciousness was created in me and then I started reexamining myself. And I started realizing the damage and the baggage I had created. And slowly, not thinking, "Well I'm just using drugs. I'm not hurting any-body." Well, you know what, realizing, the realization that I'm hurting everybody, my family, most of all, the community, the world in general. Atonement for me came with a new spirituality.

After serving six years, Shahid overcame his anger and started "thinking about his actions:"

I was about 24, 25 when that happened. That caused me to start thinking about my actions. What I understand as a man, we are accountable for our own actions. That's what caused me to start reflecting on myself, is to accept responsibility for my own actions. I believe that what society did to me, I did to myself. So that's when I started turning my life around and getting my act, how that caused me to do what I did to have this 7 to life, being with this women who really didn't care about me, but just what she wanted and how I responded to her and my desire to please. How they worked hand in hand to, in effect, lead me to where I wanted to believe in love.

Vince, a middle-class, married soldier, got involved in drugs and, out of the blue, committed a robbery that went astray. After several years, he started looking deeper into himself:

So I really started looking at the things that I do in my whole life. If I can't be at peace with myself, how could I ever expect to be at peace with other people around me? And so then I began this long and processed self-reflection. Watching what I do, whenever I do—and at first fortunately it became a very egotistical thing. I thought that oh, it's so great I can create this wall around it and be protected by all this negativity but the problem is just like sitting in the eye of this hurricane or a storm and so I had to really learn it was about me opening up and just being more open. And so I just started slowing working on who I was and I did it through meditation.

EVOLVING INTO A "GOOD PERSON"

Through the years of examining their motivations and behavior and participating in many self-help programs, these lifers have evolved into caring, thoughtful, responsible "good persons." They have acquired an understanding of their personal traits, weakness, propensities that led to them committing a serious crime and a view of society that recognizes that all people are humans worthy of respect and are interconnected and dependent on each other. This leads to the plans most of them have of engaging some social service upon release.

Jerry, after years of hostility and violence, found peace and started working with young people to prevent them from following the violent career he pursued:

> So since I've been in, my whole thing though has been, even before I came to San Quentin when I was in Calipat', my whole thing was about peace. You know what, I think if you can teach a man to live peacefully and to enjoy that peace, I mean that's best thing you can ever give a person in life. And that's what I do. When I came to San Quentin, I got with Lonnie Morris. You know Lonnie Morris, big mouth, big skinny guy? I got with him. He's real smart. We started a group called No More Tears and that's against the violence. Try and teach people to curb their violence. Started working with the kids. I've always wanted to do that. The SQUIRES. I was also working with them, I started, I had a program we had in Wasco, but it was pretty much like SQUIRES.

Richard, after years of involvement in yard activities, woke up and stopped "acting like a stupid moron," and "living like an animal" and began planning to be "intimate with people," and working with kids:

> And I want to get to really working with kids, not just with kids, because it is not about just education with kids, its about education of adults as well. You can't just educate the kids over here in some program and expect them all on their own to figure it out, so I see them just educating the kids that come in here. It's got to be the parents. The adults have to have a different mindset and understand it is not just about their job all the time, it's about listening to what's happening.

Lonnie acquired a deep understanding of justice and his role in a more just society:

> What I try to tell young people all the time is that we have no idea the impact that we have on other people's lives when we commit crimes against them. There's no such thing as a victimless crime, you know. There's no victimless crime, because I don't know that what the crime does to you. You're a person and it impacts you in ways that I can't measure when I break into your house, steal your car, any of those things these crimes, write checks. All those things have emotional, psychological connections to them and it causes people different kinds of trauma and different kinds of emotional

reality and then it even shifts people's perception about life, about how they value other human beings and their relationship to human beings. So there's so much and it's kind of a reality this so-called justice system as we call it, that we don't take into account when we're dealing with the criminal justice system that it does everyone a disservice that we don't take them into account.

Noel started seeing his actions from other people's viewpoints:

One thing I came to realize is that we all are human. We are all God's creations. There is value in life. I began seeing the value in life—people. You start looking at yourself. Would you want someone to hurt your family? Would you want somebody to rob your family? I remember onetime my mom got robbed. She never told me about it when I was on the streets. She told me after I got locked up. Someone had robbed her right there at gunpoint. I got so angry. How could someone do that to my mom. So I thought about that. And that's the way people feel. I started feeling how people feel. Soon I was realizing that this not right. That's one thing I seen. I realized that I don't have to fight. I have nothing to prove, because I'm not with that audience. When you are in that lifestyle, you think you have this audience that's always watching. That's not true. And you realize that the same audience that you are playing to when you do that stuff, there is nothing they can do for you. Its like defending a block, defending a neighborhood, defending a name of a town when you are involved in gangs. The town doesn't belong to me. The mayor of the city doesn't pay me a visit in jail and tell me that you have done a great job defending your block against a rival gang member. The town is not mine. If the town was mine and I could do what I would with it, nobody could tell me anything and then I would look at it, would I want somebody come up and paint up my block, my house, spray paint it? No, I would take care of it.

P. J. learned to understand himself and life in general through helping others in the Victim Offender program:

I think before that, up to 27 years old when I committed my crime, I had a pretty narrow view, not only in a worldly way, but also in a personal way, in a way of family and my little inner circle. It was much more limited as far as exploring into relationships and different things going on in life besides doing the things that I had to do to survive and day-to-day stuff. So the transition that I made throughout the years and I'm still working on is going deeper than the mundane things that a person has to do to go through their days and do the regular things you got to do in order to live, but going deeper into how I can understand myself better, how I can use what I learn from others to help others. Like working with the youth and doing the Victim Offender programs that I do, working with the families, mothers, fathers, brothers, and sisters of people that have been killed. They come in and have dialogues with us. We do different exercises, too. It helps us get to a deeper understanding of the other side of the crime. That is a level I have reached that is so much richer than being caught up in what I was out there—like a lot of people are, just caught up in just working, taking care of the kids, paying the bills, and buying the things that you need, things that you want. It is just so much of a richer way to interact with people on that deeper kind of level. You know, interacting with kids that are in big major trouble that are headed towards death or prison and working with people who are family members of people who were murdered, that are going through the grieving process, their healing process. Working in those kind of circles is a whole different way of living your life than doing just what you have to do to just live your life.

Rusty discovered the interconnectedness of all humans and then the responsibility we have toward each other:

What I see now is the interconnectedness of mankind, that we're all here and that we're all connected. That any actions that one person had no matter how minute they are, whether it's within your thoughts, whether it's within your words, or whether it's in your behavior, has the ability to create or has the ability to destroy. I believe that everything that happens, this interconnectedness that exists, it's like one of the ways that I can say this is for me, I had a lot of things that were in my unconscious. When I could bring those from my unconsciousness into my consciousness, OK, it created an awareness and a mindfulness that I never had before. Because of this mindfulness that existed, it compelled me to become transformed and to want to give back this same new-found knowledge and insight to others, so that they can experience the same thing. I can say it like this, that I'm creating my experience so I can experience my creations. One level that it exists for everyone else when they can address themselves in this way and as a counseling tool, I find that in a cognitive restructuring, which is a key technique in the addiction field that completely changes someone's thinking and their belief system, and I believe for me that's been a big part of me because it was this flawed belief system and this flawed thinking and my addictive state that led me down the path that I am in now that I derived from the prison. And now with the revelations and the insights that I've gained now, I believe that rather than do violence on someone else I would probably end up being a victim now.

PLANS FOR LIFE AFTER RELEASE

Most of the lifers who experienced a transformation and sought atonement for their crimes and past dissolute and irresponsible lives plan to engage in public service activities upon their release. Most of them have had some involvement with youth through the programs, such as SQUIRES, in which youth in trouble are brought to the prison for counseling. Also, the lifers consider themselves experts on youth crime because they were involved in "getting into trouble" and crime when they were young. Consequently, they plan to continue working with kids when they get out of prison.

Albert would rather work with kids than do another job paying much more:

> I'm ready to throw in these blues and put on a suit and tie and go do what I got to do, you know what I mean? Have fun doing that. I told the board that too, you know. I said I like working with these kids and youth. And if working with the youth programs like Real Choices in San Francisco or San Mateo, or anywhere for that matter in the Bay Area, paid me less money than what I would be earning as translator for immigration department or any other county firm, I would feel good doing that, you know. I would live free doing that. I like doing that period. And you know the reward is when the youth counselors say man, thank you Al, thank you man, thank you.

Bryan wants to continue college, obtain a Master's degree in marriage and family therapy:

> Well I, I have some unique stuff going on I think. I've completed the academic portions to become certified as a drug counselor in California and in June I'm going to take the written exam. I'm practicing. We're doing internships. We're practicing to become drug counselors. We've set up the programs here. Also, I'm a facilitator in a male accountability group but, I really enjoy working with other people either individually or in group settings. And

so I think I might pursue a Master's degree in marriage and family therapy or some kind of psychology degree or sociology. I'm very interested in sociology.

Bobby is willing to work as a drug and alcohol counselor for no pay:

> I want to be a drug and alcohol counselor. I want to work in the center for substance abuse, both adolescent and adults, you know. I don't mind giving it free. I like to go to the church and offer my skills in the church, 'cause I know plumbing and I know machinist work. I don't really like doing it, carpentry and stuff like that, so I like to go in that and offer my time. Yeah, just get out and live.

Jerry uses his experience and knowledge to accomplish positive change with young people:

> Well, I've always had, I think, strong parole plans because, like I said, once I started, I got my focus straight. I knew exactly what it is I wanted to do. I wanted to, like I said, same thing I do in San Quentin allow me to do. But I see them to start turn the wheels in another direction on that too. I wanted to accomplish a positive change out there in the community for people, young men coming up like I came up and no one was there to say hey, that's not right don't do it like that. This is what that's gonna lead you to. I wanted to accomplish a change like that and so what I did I was gonna work with, take the program I got, No More Tears, out there to curb violence, detrimental behavior, implement that into the community.

Lonnie describes his desire to work with kids and his unique abilities for this type of endeavor:

> At this point in my life, I can make the case that I'd be much more of value in society working with young people, working with gangbangers, working with thugs, working with dope fiends, working with prostitutes, working with people that I know have come from that lifestyle, working with those people to try to help them change and transform their lives than I can ever do here. Because I'm doing that work here now that I could do on a much broader scale with more tools and resources at my disposal than I can sitting here in prison and dying off as a voice that may never get heard to the degree that people being hurt. That's the tragedy of this. I'm just one of a thousand guys who make these kind of transformations that now really can be soldiers for change. We can go out there now and say, "Hey, man you know what? I've

done it." You got this big flap going about hip-hop as a result of this Don Innis thing right? Well they're not gonna listen to certain people. I'm talking hood kids and kids from the ghetto the hood gangstas they call them. They're not gonna listen to certain people telling them about, "Oh, you need to change your lyrics and you need to contain your misogynistic attitudes and victimization." They don't hear that. They hear it from somebody like me say, "Hold up man, what you talking about? Check this out, let me run this by you, partner," and give it to them straight up. Because I've done it. I know what it is. I lived it, you know. I can tell 'em that it ain't nothing gangsta about being gangsta. Ain't nothing keeping it real about keeping it gangsta. I can let them know these things coming from a real live person who said, "Man, look I wasted 30 years of my life trying to live that role you playing. And the consequence, you have no idea what the consequences of your actions are gonna garner later in life. You just see what you see right now you can't see what I see 'cause you haven't been through what I've been through." So there's guys like me throughout the state who can go out there and deliver that message, deliver it authentically and get the kind of response that will help young people change their thinking about who they are, what they are, and what they want to be. And we need that in our society and if they don't give us an opportunity to do those things, it speaks to what did our society really say about what we want to be as human beings? About what we value. Retribution becomes more important than transformation and rehabilitation? And that's the question I ask everybody. So that's me.

German, after years of experience with SQUIRES, wants to do community service upon release:

Yes, the SQUIRES some of the guys that they bring in, they're already doing time at the boys' ranch. In fact, they bring kids where they were from San Francisco where I did time in the boys' ranch, these same kids like myself. They never brought me to no place like this. But I saw that and I'm really passionate about helping the kids. That's really in my heart like this program here that my whole purpose is to just get educated to use that to help these kids. You know but I have to, you know. I have options when I leave this place I have different job offers. I can be a counselor, a drug substance abuse counselor and also working with at risk youth. But I just want to do that as a career, to be able to work with these kids and have kids so that they don't do what I did and they don't end up like me and that's my whole thing that's my sort of what's holding me, one of the things that I did to my community and my society and that's really in my heart but I'm also certified electrician. I can, you know, work as an electrician. I mean I have different options, but I want to do community service, you know.

Julius, who has had some vocational education, but has more interest in teaching bible class and considerable training in counseling youth, plans to continue to "spread the word" and work with kids:

When I get out 'cause I'm planning on working with kids you know that's my whole thing right now. I might be working with kids or I might just be going some place and hook up with some church and tell me to go and spread the gospel. I might just live like that I don't know what God's plan is. I can only go one day at a time. So that's why I'm led to do when I get out that's what I do. But I do have plans. I do have jobs. I have all that, you know. That's not a problem. I can—you open the door for me right now I got a job to go to.

Noel plans to go home and take care of his aging parents who stuck by him through his years of imprisonment:

My plans when I get out is to live with my mother and my father. Not because I don't have any other place to live, but because they have taken care of me throughout my incarceration. One thing you come to realize when you're incarcerated. See when you live the life involved in this code or culture of the streets, you develop a new family, street family. You always have the family you were born into, your mother, your father, your siblings. And when you get incarcerated, in trouble, the street family only cares about you when you're there with them and you're providing for them. I mean you're putting into the pot, drinking, smoking, supplying drugs, and cars. But when you get locked up, your mother, your father, they're the ones that come and visit you, send you care packages. They send you money. Your homeboys, homegirls, they, very rarely. I think I've had one, only one ever sent me some money. That's when you start realizing you have a real family. And that's why my plan is to go back and take care of my mom and my dad, because they are elderly. My dad's 81, my mom's 80. My dad's in great health, strong. My mother, she's had bypass surgery, she's had a stroke, but she's doing alright. But I want to be there to provide for them. Through this incarceration, I've developed skills. I have my AA degree and I want to be able to go higher. But I've also developed skills in the sheet metal trade, journeyman skills. I can get a job right away—25, 30 dollars an hour. That's my plan. Going to live with them, provide for them. If possible someway, somehow, get back into school, shoot for my BA and my ultimate goal is to get a PhD in sociology because I work a lot with people, people stuck in the same place I came from—violent streets.

In addition to trying to go through the "healing process" with his family, particularly with his two sons who are both in prison now, P. J. wants to continue youth counseling, an activity that has been important to him in prison:

The things I am going to spend most of my energy on when I get out is really just spending quality time with my family, my parents who are sick, whose days are numbered, especially my dad. And trying to help my two boys who are in prison right now. And really trying to go through the healing process that we need to go through, especially my boys, whose dad left, abandoned them, basically at two and eight years old and they ended up in a not very good situation at all. Their home environment changed from pretty darn good to pretty bad. So there is a lot of healing that needs to go on there, between me and them. I'm sure that is some of the reason they are in the trouble they are in now. One was going to get out but they put another violent charge on him that happened before he got arrested for the first one. He's looking at a third strike right now. My youngest boy, he's 21 right now. I've got him some help and I think he is going to get two years instead of 25 to life. The strike is weak. I don't think it will stick, anyway. So I am pretty sure he will be able to get a deal for two years. My other boy is looking at three and a half, my 28-year-old. They were doing pretty good till they got into some trouble in their teens. I actually got them in here to go to the SQUIRES program, the youth program. I got permission from the warden, Calderon, when he used to be here. My older boy was 17, my younger was 11 at the time. My oldest boy, the worst thing he did was steal a car. He had gotten into some violent stuff. So I got him the OK to come in here with the SQUIRES and he did a 180. He stopped getting into trouble. And my 11-year-old was doing pretty good but I just wanted both of them to come and do the SQUIRES together. It worked for quite a while, for a few years and then the big turnaround for my oldest boy when he was almost 23. I got my first date from the board and then I got the call that the governor had taken my date and I am back at square one again. It was less than a week later that my son picked up a pretty heavy violent crime and he did his first sentence in prison. He did two years. And this is the third time he is back, now. He's real good out there. He is motivated. He works in construction. I hooked him up with some contractors. He hangs sheetrock. He does good for awhile and then he will slip away. He doesn't have anybody, a solid role model to stick with him when he gets kinda weak and then he will start to drink and that goes to drugs and it's just a matter of time. Both of my boys are into that now.

There are two different at risk youth agencies that told me I am hired when I get out because they have brought kids in here for years and they see how I work with kids. So I am definitely going to continue on with the youth counseling and I am also a carpenter and a plumber. I've got jobs out there with people I've known all these years who I have worked for before I came to prison and who are still friends of mine who are going to employ me.

Richard wants to work with kids and adults, to bring people together, and create new communities:

And I want to get to really working with kids, not just with kids, because it is not about just education with kids, its about education of adults as well. You can't just educate the kids. Over here is some program and expect them all on their own to figure it out. So I see them just educating the kids that come in here, it's got to be the parents. The adults have to have a different mindset and understand it is not just about their job all the time, it's about listening to what's happening. The terrible tragedy that had to transpire over there in Virginia. Where this man was crying out, please help me, please help me. Like when I was a 12-year-old kid and I was yelling out, please help me. When I my cousin whipped my ass. Well, sucked it up. It was wrong that he acted out like that and it was wrong I acted out like I did. I'm not gonna say I'm better or worse, because you know man I messed up just like him in a different way. The thing is though, the thing we've got to do is be like stewards, ambassadors. Get our asses together, get our rumps out there and start ₁ aying attention to people. Get in them areas, get in them neighborhoods, and start working with, not only the kids, the adults as well. Get amusements going at the parks. Get meetings going with police departments, crime control department, the child protective agency, and all these other people. Get a unit, somehow, going on, because that is what it is going to take. It's going to take us binding together as human beings and working together as a team. There isn't no I in a team. And that's a fact. And that's what I'm doing. That's what I'm educating myself for.

But it's time to let Richard to go home, not only home, but in the society so I can be, ah, tantamount to rescue kids, to rescue grownups, and to clean up some areas that need to be cleaned up and to help some people that need to be helped. There's people out there that can't go out and mow their lawn. They don't have enough strength. There some old folks that need some help, need their house painted or just go over and sit with them, make them some coffee, and sit there and talk to them. And that's what I want to do, man. And I want to take that and pass it on to someone else. So they can have some things that are great. No one wants to listen to the old folks anymore. But that's what I want to do. I want to sit there and say heh, let me rub your feet and talk to you. That's my reparation for the degradation I brought on to, not only me but to so many people.

Rusty, who has had extensive training in alcohol and drug treatment, has his post-prison plans well thought out:

I've got short-term goals and I've got long-term goals. My short-term goal will be getting my feet back on the ground and renewing connections with family members and further making it at home, being able to be there and to allow my behavior and my actions speak to what I have been saying for years so that they can see that I am a changed person. Because all they know from here is who I am now. Initially, I want to serve as an alcohol counselor or in a related field, maybe as an interventionist. I'm not sure. Long term, I want to start a "Clean and Sober" living house. I want to go from there utilizing housing from Urban Development and get an auctioned, either a nursing home that is out of business or a motel, and I want convert it to an active treatment center.

Shahid wants to help other people understand their emotions and their pain and in this way help them mend as he was able to mend himself:

I understand how we affect younger people by our actions. What I understand about myself, what I understand about my actions, that other people think as I used to think, but teaches me to understand their emotions, how they feel and not dealing with your pain, how in the end it can be used against you until it can become self-destructive. My future is to help people to mend and understand their lives, help them to understand their actions, not only their lives, but their actions. Give back, discuss my case with people, do not allow my shame to forbid me to bare my soul. I'm going to become a drug counselor and through drug counseling, addiction, because you can't look at addiction as just drugs. Addiction is a lot of different things. People can be addicted to satisfying their own desires. What is the cost of satisfying your own desires? What would it get you, what are your reasons, why do you desire what you desire? I want to help people to think about their actions, understanding what motivates you. I didn't understand what motivated me to be who I was and now I do.

THE INNOCENT

The three lifers who claim and appear to be innocent, though they resent their imprisonment, have maintained a positive attitude and positive plans for the future. Rachman, who has served 25 years, stated that imprisonment was "the best thing that ever happened to him," in spite of the fact that he is innocent:

The worst thing that ever could have happened to me is what these people did to me. By falsely accusing me and convicting me of a crime that I never committed. That's the worst thing ever could have happened to me. But listen to this. But the best thing that ever happened to me was me coming to prison. I want people to understand I found myself in here. I graduated from college. I met my wife in here. She's my best friend. I teach school in here, tutor reading program in here. I helped graduate more people in that GE program than the education program with GED. Some cats walk with me on the line and say, they say, "Rachman don't you remember me? I'm the one you helped get his GED." That's the best thing that could have happened to me, me coming in here. It saved my life, you know. I probably won't tell them detectives that though for falsely accusing me. But deep down inside, I thanked them. I do. I want to get out. Sometime I look at the news and I say, well I'm cool but then I want to get out 'cause I got a wife now and my wife she's, her first husband, he died, so she had these sons that I help raised, it turns out. We got married, we been married almost 20 years and I raised those kids.

Marvin, who was raised in orphanages and foster care homes, developed a thorough understanding of his and his mother's problem:

> I think I've been fairly successful at the introspection that I needed to do in order to find out how come things happened and to assign responsibility where it correctly belongs and to un-assign it from places where it didn't belong. I now know that I blamed my mother for a lot of things, for having to go to foster care that I know now that she had her own problems. I know now that she was stuck in a cycle of abuse from different marriages, that she was profoundly damaged. I know now that she came from overseas and was placed in an orphanage after her family was killed during the world war. I know now that she was scarred without anybody to help her process that through and I don't think she was ready at her young age to have children and I think that that's why we were eventually made wards of the state. I was made a ward of the state by the time I was four years old and years of abusive foster placements left me emotionally scarred and alienated. So trying to process through that kind of thing by your-self and not understanding the mechanisms is part of the major problem that men here run into. And these are men who don't have anywhere near the ability that I had to go out and research these things as much as you can. I don't know that the science that they have available is all correct. I think a lot of it, a lot of that psychiatric, psychological theory is just that, it's theory and a lot of it is mumbo jumbo. I don't think that you do things 'cause you weren't potty trained right when you were a child. But I do think that there's a profound impact on people who are tied to their bed or were whipped or were beaten. I think that there're repercus-sions to that and I think that if you don't work through that it affects your later life. So how in a system like this you come in with this type of scar and not be able to process it. Or if you do try to process it, you have to realize that it will affect your chances of ever getting out of prison because of course if you're abused as a child, we can't let you out. And that's what's ridiculous.

Upon release, he wants to reform childcare services:

> I want to go out and save the children. What I do want to do, if I get a chance, is reform foster care. I do want to try and work on the system. I want to, of course, help those people that are within in my range to help at the moment that I'm there to help. I'm not going to go out and make that my life's vocation because I think that

there's a bigger thing that has to happen. The board then asks what it is that I want to do the most and I tell them it's usually, you know, that I'd like to just spend the first year with my wife and reacquaint myself with my free-self and with my family and then from there I want to go out and try and work with individuals that are coming out of the system that need to somebody to meet them at the gate you know, need somebody to be there to help them process.

He adds that he would like to honor his wife and enjoy some of the things he never experienced:

I never had the chance to enjoy the beach or eat in a restaurant or buy my wife an anniversary present, give her a flower. I'm talking about in a traditional way where you're honoring the person who has honored you with a faithful heart and myself as a man. I just feel I need to give that to my wife. I'm her cover. I'm the person that is supposed to be there for her and instead she's here for me and it reeks havoc with both of our lives.

Watani, who upon his escape lived in Surinam for 20 years where he had 6 children, writes, lives for his family, and hopes to get out to be with them before he dies.

I have been back for 13 years. Writing has become my passion now. My main focus was on my family, trying to get them over here, stay in touch with them, communication, you know. I've met a lot of good people since I've been here. They've really been a lifeline. Trying to get medicine. So the first few years I have been focusing on them. At the same time writing, trying to tell my story. People at UCLA, a professor, Scott Brown, is writing a journal, suppose to come out in a journal in American Studies. I've been writing to a lot of universities, most of the universities, trying to relate the issues of that period to the students, trying to have a dialogue.

The main thing now is trying to reconnect with my children. Recently, I realized now how much damage has been done to them. I thought that when they are here now. I didn't know what they what had been done to them. They were practically abandoned. Their mother had another breakdown and she started using drugs and they were left on their own and so they got separated in different parts of Surinam on their own. I talked to my son and I had no idea. My son, Sahib, and his wife have the children, and they sat down and talked to my son and he said that if it had of been him he would have never abandoned his children the way I did and that was something that was so poignant to me. That was something I didn't realize the damage that took place as a result of my leaving them, really a lot of anger in terms of abandonment. Anyway, my son, he's right there. He's communication director in the county. He's been there for quite awhile. His wife teaches school. My oldest kid, I have a daughter going to Westville College, she'll be going to UCLA after next semester. She is 20. My oldest, she's 22, another one, she's 18, 16, 14, and 13. There's one or two years' difference in their ages. They're trying to fit in, a little too fast, into society. The one that is in school, she has a dream, and I think she is going to succeed, of going back to Surinam and becoming the first woman president. I have some good ones and then I have my youngest daughter and my son who is having a little problem. My daughter, everything in society, she is trying to be part of it, get into it. She's not listening. My oldest son, he is into the gang thing, he has homies now. They came to see me last month. They all live in LA, except for my daughter, she's living on campus. Westville is not too far from Fresno. They're all having their struggles, adjustments, you know. I try to be there for them, listen to them. They talk, say things, and I listen to them. You know, it makes things a whole lot easier.

*   *   *

These 17 men, all of whom have served many more years than prescribed by California sentencing laws and Administrative Regulations, have made a remarkable transformation. This is a small sample, but my experience with lifers over the many years I have studied prisons, which has included my associating with hundreds of lifers, convinces me that they represent most lifers. In the essential characteristics, their crimes are like most lifers' crimes. And given the opportunities, most lifers make similar transformations.

6

CALIFORNIA LIFERS' LEGAL PREDICAMENT

The 17 lifers in my sample, as well as most of the more than 10,000 other lifers who are eligible for parole and who have served many years beyond their prescribed sentences, have been held far beyond that required by the goals of imprisonment—retribution, deterrence, incapacitation, and rehabilitation. This is occurring at a great financial cost to the society and an emotional cost in terms of the tremendous pain experienced by the lifers and harm to their families. In this chapter, we will examine how and why this expensive injustice is being executed by the government functionaries who determine lifers' sentences.

The California Board of Prison Terms (BPT) sets lifers' sentences according to Penal Code 3041. The Code reads:

(a) In the case of any inmate sentenced pursuant to any provision of law, other than Chapter 4.5 (commencing with Section 1170) of Title 7 of Part 2, the Board of Parole Hearings shall meet with each inmate during the third year of incarceration for the purposes of reviewing the inmate's file, making recommendations, and documenting activities and conduct pertinent to granting or withholding post conviction credit. One year prior to the inmate's minimum eligible parole release date a panel of two or more commissioners or deputy commissioners shall again meet with the inmate and *shall normally* set a parole release date as provided in Section 3041.5.

(b) The panel or the board, sitting en banc, shall set a release date unless it determines that the gravity of the current convicted offense or offenses, or the timing and gravity of current or past convicted offense or offenses, is such that consideration of the public safety requires a more lengthy period of incarceration for this individual, and that a parole date, therefore, cannot be fixed. (Emphasis added.)

In addition, a referendum passed by California voters in 1988 gave the state's governor veto power over all paroles granted to persons convicted of first or second degree homicide.

As described in Chapter 1, the parole board established matrices to guide parole boards in determining lifers' sentences. These matrices take into account a variety of factors, such as whether the victim participated in the criminal act or whether there was severe trauma or torture, or a threat to public order. The recommended sentences according to the matrix for first degree homicide range from 25 to 33 years. Considering the reduction of the sentence for good behavior, which is one-third off if a prisoner does not "lose" good time credits through disciplinary action, the recommended sentences for first degree homicide range from 16.77 to 22 years. The corrected range for second degree homicide is 10 to 14 years.

As pointed out in Chapter 1, before 1985 prisoners convicted for first degree homicide were receiving sentences below the lowest recommended sentence in these matrices. Then, after the punitive swing reshaped penology, particularly sentencing policy, sentences leaped up and now most second degree homicides result in sentences of 20 to 30 years and first degree 27 to 35 years.

This is a dramatic shift. The official justification for this shift is that the various sentencing functionaries have become more concerned with public safety and are therefore denying parole by following section (b) of PC 3041 that instructs them to set sentences *unless* they determine that prisoners being considered for parole pose a threat to public safety. They continue to use this reason for denying parole to prisoners, year after year, no matter what evidence the prisoners bring to their hearings that they have made great efforts to rehabilitate themselves and are remorseful for their crimes.

It is my and many other observers' opinion that the shift is actually a manifestation of the new punitive ideology that now dominates penal policy. The shift in penal ideology and the resultant changes in sentencing policy are dramatically reflected in two California court cases: *In re Dennis Stanworth on Habeas Corpus* and *In re John E. Dannenberg on Habeas Corpus.*[41] In 1966, Stanworth was sentenced to death following his plea of guilty to two counts of 1st degree murder. He also pled guilty to kidnapping, forcible rape, oral copulation, and robbery. The death penalty was set aside when the California Supreme Court, following the United States Supreme Court in Furman, found the death penalty to be "impermissibly cruel." Stanworth become "parolable" under the existing indeterminate sentencing law.

Stanworth appeared before the Adult Authority, the parole board under the indeterminate sentence system, in 1974, 1976, and 1977 and each time was denied parole. He appeared before the BPT, the parole board under the new sentencing law, and was denied a parole in 1977 and 1978. In 1979, he was found ready for parole and given a total adjusted term of 23 years, 4 months. In granting his parole, the BPT stressed the following factors:

> (1) lack of prior serious criminal history or history of violent conduct; (2) institutional behavior, including cell study even while on death row, excellent work record, obtaining an associate of arts degree and a certificate in data processing, and six years of participation in therapy programs; (3) defendant's only disciplinary infraction occurred 10 years before while he was on death row; (4) no psychiatric contraindications (the reports of several psychotherapists who had worked closely with defendant in prison were uniformly laudatory); (5) realistic parole plans, including a $12,000 irrevocable educational trust fund set up in his behalf, and a personal $3,000 savings account.[42]

Stanworth appealed the length of this sentence to the trial court on the grounds that it was reached by mechanical computation according to the new matrix and not by individualized consideration that was required by the indeterminate sentencing law under which he was sentenced. The trial court ruled in his favor. In appeal, the Supreme Court of California upheld the trial court's decision. Stanworth was released after serving 17 years. The Supreme Court commented:

> The Authority does not fix that period pursuant to a formula of punishment, but in accordance with the adjustment and social rehabilitation of the individual analyzed as a human composite of intellectual, emotional and genetic factors.[43]

---

41 *In re Dennis Stanworth on Habeas Corpus,* 33 Cal. 3rd 176 and *In re Dannenberg,* p. 1061.
42 *In re Stanworth,* p. 179.
43 Ibid., p. 182.

John Dannenberg was found guilty of second degree murder of his wife in 1986. He appeared before the BPT in 1996, 1997, and 1999 and the board declined to set a parole date. They based these denials on his unsuitability for parole because of the nature of his crime, which they stated indicated that he would be a threat to public safety if released and because he failed to accept full responsibility for his crime.

Dannenberg petitioned the Superior Court of Marin County and the court found no basis for the board's determination that Dannenberg was unsuitable on the grounds of public safety. The court wrote:

> Dannenberg had no criminal history and had shown remorse for his wife's death. His prison record and post-release plans were exemplary. Prison psychologists found no mental or emotional disorder, and there was no evidence he needed therapy. Nor could unsuitability be based on the nature of the commitment offense itself, because there was no evidence that Dannenberg's crime was callous and cruel, or indifferent to human suffering, beyond any and all second degree murders.[44]

The court ordered the board to conduct a new hearing and recommend a sentence length of 17, 18, or 19 years.

The State appealed the court's decision to the Court of Appeal of the First Appellate District:

> The Court of Appeal affirmed insofar as the order granted the inmate's habeas corpus petition and directed the board to promptly conduct another parole suitability hearing, but reversed insofar as the order directed the board to reach a particular result in the absence of changed circumstances.[45]

The California Supreme Court accepted the case. In a long and convoluted argument, they rejected an earlier Court of Appeal's decision in which the court had stated that "the Board's (The BPT) authority to make an exception based on the gravity of a life term, inmate's current or past offenses should not operate so as to swallow the rule that parole is 'normally' to be granted. Otherwise, the Board's case-by-case rulings would destroy the proportionality contemplated by section 3041 (the sentencing law)."[46] The Supreme Court ruling on Dannenberg's appeal concluded that the words "shall normally" mean neither shall nor

---

44 *In re Dannenberg*, p. 1076.
45 *In re John E. Dannenberg on Habeas Corpus*, 102 Cal. App. 4th 95.
46 *In re Thomas Ramirez on Habeas Corpus*, 94 Cal. App. 4th 549.

normally and said that the gravity of offense may indicate unsuitability for parole because it suggests that the person may be a continued threat to public safety.

> *Section 3041* does not require the Board to schedule such an inmate's release when it reasonably believes the gravity of the commitment offense indicates a continuing danger to the public, simply to ensure that the length of the inmate's confinement will not exceed that of others who committed similar crimes.
>
> Our conclusion in this regard is confirmed when we read the language of *section 3041* in its statutory context. Other provisions governing parole decisions for indeterminate life prisoners— adopted both before and after enactment of *section 3041*— buttress the notion that the determination of suitability for parole involves a paramount assessment of the public safety risk posed by the particular offender, without regard to a comparative analysis of similar offenses committed by other persons.[47]

The difference in the courts' reasoning about the statutory language in Stanworth and Dannenberg is astonishing. It is important to note that the composition of the California Supreme Court had changed dramatically. Rose Bird and two other "liberal" judges had been removed. The court had been packed with conservatives appointed by conservative governors. The old court upheld the beliefs related to the rehabilitative ideal that had been the basis of the statutes governing release on parole. Mainly, defendants were changeable and redeemable. The perspective of the new court reflects the new punitive mood: criminals are different from decent people, are likely to be permanently committed to crime, should be incapacitated for long periods, and deserve severe punishment. For serious crimes, such as murder, they should be incapacitated and punished by holding them for very long periods, even life, regardless of the laws in effect at the time of the crime. However, except for highly inappropriate and blatantly illegal public declarations such as that made by Governor Davis, when he stated that he would hold all persons convicted of murder for life, parole board members and court judges must couch their punitiveness in "respectable" legalese. This was what the Supreme Court did in the case of Dannenberg and does in many of the cases that have come before it in recent years.

The idea that Dannenberg's crime can be used as evidence that he is

---

47 *In re Dannenberg*, p. 1084.

any more of a threat to public safety than anyone else who has been convicted of a second degree murder and has spent 20 years in prison is silly. In the first place, his homicide was an ordinary second degree murder. Dannenberg was:

> drawing a bath for his son when he noticed debris in the drain that could cause a clog. He produced a pipe wrench and a screwdriver to fix a leaky toilet valve. "During this time, he evidently said something to his wife about the drain." She came into the bathroom and picked up the screwdriver. A heated argument ensued. Screaming that she "wanted him dead," the victim jabbed the screwdriver at Dannenberg, cutting his arm, and clawed and scratched his forearm with her fingernails. Dannenberg first tried to defend himself with his bare hands. Then he picked up the pipe wrench and hit the victim once on the side of the head. When she continued to advance on him, he "hit her a couple more times on the head," and she fell to the floor. Dannenberg himself collapsed "and may have passed out."[48]

He testified to the following additional details:

> As both he and the victim collapsed on the floor, the victim was lying on her back, still holding the screwdriver, and Dannenberg was kneeling over her, pinning her arms. She seemed to relax, but then suddenly placed her feet against his shoulders and pushed. He was knocked back against the bathroom door and fell to the floor. After that, he remembered nothing until he saw the victim lying on the edge of the tub. A pool of blood covered the floor where she had previously lain. There was also considerable blood on her head and smeared on the wall. Dannenberg could not move at first, because his legs, curled underneath him, were asleep. From his low position, and in a dazed condition, he did not notice the victim's head was in the water. Eventually he reached over and tried to take her pulse, but could not feel anything. He then struggled to his feet, went to his bedroom, and called 911.[49]

This is obviously an ordinary second degree murder, one, in fact, in which the victim initiated the violent encounter. This would place the crime in a category in the matrix established by the paroling authorities calling for a sentence of 16, 17, or 18 years.

---

48 Ibid., pp. 1072–73.
49 Ibid., p. 1073.

In his dissent to the majority opinion in Dannenberg, Justice Moreno counters the reasoning of the majority:

> Second degree murder, of which John E. Dannenberg stands convicted, is by its very nature a serious crime. But as explained below, the relevant statute mandates that people convicted of second degree murder be considered for and normally granted parole. At the very least, the statute mandates that the Board of Prison Terms (Board) not deny parole solely because the prisoner has committed the murder. Yet the majority's decision today would permit the Board to do precisely that. And though the majority does so in the name of public safety and individualized parole decisions, the majority opinion in fact advances neither goal. Rather, the position the majority adopts requires the judicial rubber stamping of the Board's decisions, no matter how unfounded or unjust they might be.[50]

Justice Moreno also points out that the majority's interpretation of the sentencing law's terms "shall normally" could lead to virtually all paroles being denied:

> the majority concludes that *section 3041(a)'s* statement that the Board "shall *normally* set a parole release date . . . in a manner that will provide *uniform terms for offenses of similar gravity and magnitude* in respect to their threat to the public" has no real meaning, and is nothing more than a "legislative assumption, or hope, that uniform release dates would be a typical or common result."
>
> [. . .]
>
> What the majority does not and cannot explain is why the Legislature should go through the trouble of describing extensively a method of granting parole that the Board "shall" carry out if this statute expresses—very uncharacteristically for a Legislature—nothing more than a "hope."[51] (Emphasis original.)

Dannenberg was a 46-year-old, middle-class, educated professional who had *no* criminal record. At the time of this last court decision, he was in his early sixties. He had an unblemished prison record and made many positive contributions to prison community—"being a helpful resource to other prisoners and prison staff, fixing the electrical wiring

---

50 Ibid., pp. 1103–04.
51 Ibid., p. 1101.

at San Quentin, and volunteering with an inmate education advisory committee and a Jewish religious group for prisoners."[52] The board's decision to deny him parole and the upholding of this decision on the grounds that he is unsuitable for release because his crime indicates that he is a future threat to public safety reveals the hypocrisy and arbitrariness of the board and the court.

It also strongly suggests that some other dominant, unstated reasons are operating in sentencing decisions. As I argued above, these are, first, the extreme punitiveness of the new conservative functionaries who fill the key positions in the process—the parole board members, judges, and governors. (Governor Davis openly revealed his punitiveness.) A second reason is the fear that they will be held responsible in the public's mind for releasing someone who does commit a publicized horrible crime. Judge Robert F. Moody, who had been assigned to hear writs of habeas corpus filed in Monterey County, made this point in an article in the *Monterey Herald* titled "Politics Contribute to Parole Sham:"

> I think the problem stems in part from the Willie Horton situation, where former Massachusetts Gov. Michael Dukakis, in the midst of his 1988 campaign for president, was shown to have been involved in the release of a life-with-possibility-of-parole inmate who later raped a Maryland woman and beat her boyfriend. This was politically devastating to Dukakis, regardless of whether he was personally culpable.
>
> Since then all governors who bear parole responsibilities have been heavily scrutinized by their political opponents to see if they could be blamed for the criminal acts of any lifer parolee who did something awful after receiving a grant of parole that the governor could have prevented or overturned.
>
> All the governors of California of all political stripes since then, and the parole boards they have appointed, have been increasingly unwilling to permit release of life crime inmates, regardless of the merits of individual cases. That is understandable in a way because in practical terms, the system makes the governor politically responsible for everything the released inmates may do. This is unfair, and it is not my intention to criticize the individual governors. This approach, however, is having a devastating impact upon the integrity of the justice system and upon the administration of the prisons themselves.[53]

---

52 Ibid., p. 1076.
53 "Commentary," section E, *Monterey Herald*, October 14, 2007, p. E2.

The decision in Dannenberg is not unique, but is characteristic of the vast majority of decisions the BPT, the governor, and the California Supreme Court have made in the last few years. These decision-makers have denied parole to almost every defendant appearing before them, even though they have served many years, sometimes 10 to 15 years over the time recommended by the matrices. In addressing a habeas corpus petition filed by Arthur Criscione, the Superior Court of California, County of Santa Clara reviewed all the decisions of the BPT in the parole hearings of inmates convicted of first and second degree murder in the months of August, September, and October of 2002; July, August, September, October, November, and December of 2003; January and February of 2004; February of 2005; and January of 2006, adding up to a total of 2,690 cases decided in a total of 13 months.[54] In 100 percent of the cases, the board found the commitment offense to be "especially heinous, atrocious or cruel," a factor that indicated unsuitability for release under Title 15, 2402 (c) (1). The Santa Clara County Superior Court found that:

> Because it makes no effort to distinguish the applicability of the criteria between one case and another, the Board is able to force every case of murder into one or more of the categories contained in 2402 (c).
>
> For example, if the inmate's actions result in an instant death the Board finds that it was done in a "dispassionate and calculated manner, such as an execution-style murder." At the same time the Board finds that a murder not resulting in near instant death shows a "callous disregard for human suffering" without any further analysis or articulation of facts which justify that conclusion. If a knife or blunt object was used, the victim was "abused, defiled, or mutilated." If a gun was used the murder was performed in a "dispassionate and calculated manner, such as an execution-style murder." If bare hands were used to extinguish another human life then the crime is "particularly heinous and atrocious."
>
> Similarly, if several acts, spanning some amount of time, were necessary for the murder the Board may deny parole because the inmate had "opportunities to stop" but did not. However if the murder was accomplished quickly parole will be denied because it was done in a dispassionate and calculated manner and the victim

---

54 *In re Arthur Criscione on Habeas Corpus.* Superior Court of California, County of Santa Clara, August 30, 2007.

never had a chance to defend themselves or flee. If the crime occurred in public, or with other people in the vicinity, it has been said that the inmate "showed a callous disregard" or "lack of respect" for the "community." However if the crime occurs when the victim is found alone it could be said that the inmate's actions were aggravated because the victim was isolated and more vulnerable.

In this manner, under the Board's cursory approach, every murder has been found to fit within the unsuitability criteria. What this reduces to is nothing less than a denial of parole for the very reason the inmates are present before the Board—i.e. they committed murder. It is circular reasoning, or in fact no reasoning at all, for the Board to begin each hearing by stating the inmate is before them for parole consideration, having passed the minimum eligible parole date based on a murder conviction, and for the Board to then conclude that parole will be denied because the inmate committed acts that amount to nothing more than the minimum necessary to convict them of that crime.[55]

Justice Moreno, in his dissent in Dannenberg, made the same point:

How is the Board to determine what facts constitute a particularly egregious murder? How is the court to review that determination? The majority gives us no clue, because the concept of a crime being "more than minimally necessary to convict [a prisoner] of the offense for which he is confined" is essentially meaningless. Second degree murder is an abstraction that consists of certain legal elements. Particular second degree murders have *facts* that fit within these elements. These facts are never "necessary" or "minimally necessary" to convict someone of a second degree murder, because we can always imagine other facts that would also lead to a second degree murder conviction. Furthermore, these facts, because they are facts about a second degree murder, will almost invariably involve the defendant acted violently, cruelly, and, if acting out of provocation, greatly out of proportion to the provocation (otherwise the defendant would have been convicted of manslaughter or exonerated through self-defense). If the Board labels a second degree murder "especially callous and cruel" and exhibiting "an exceptionally callous disregard for

---

55 Ibid., pp. 13–14.

human suffering," then recites the facts of the case, is there any way for a court to review that finding and, on occasion, to find it untrue? The majority provides no explicit answer. Its implicit answer appears to be "no."[56]

The Supreme Court of the United States has ruled that lifers sentenced under laws, such as that in California in which life is not mandated, have a constitutional "liberty interest:"

> Two United States Court decisions, *Greenholtz v. Inmates of Nebraska Penal and Correctional Complex* (442 U.S. 1, 12) decided in 1979 and *Board of Pardons v. Allen* (482 U.S. 337–381) decided in 1987, held the federal due process clause creates a constitutional liberty interest for convicted persons in certain jurisdictions. The existence of this right depends on whether the state employs "mandatory language" indicating parole will be granted if certain findings are made.[57]

This means that non-arbitrary, impartial due process must be followed in setting sentences. California Penal Code sections 3041 (a) and 3041 (b) spell out how this due process should operate. PC 3041 (a) states that the board panel shall meet with the inmate, *shall normally* set a parole release date, and shall do so in a manner that will provide uniform terms for offenses of similar gravity. PC 3041 (b) states that the board shall set a release date *unless* the gravity of the offense or offenses is such that consideration of the public safety requires a more lengthy period of incarceration for this individual, and that a parole date, therefore, cannot be fixed at this meeting.

In effect, the parole board, in its decisions over the last few years, has set aside the instruction "shall normally set a parole release date" by letting an expansive interpretation of 3041 (b) supersede this instruction in virtually all cases. In doing this, it has ignored the intent of the legislature by considering *all* murders sufficiently grave or egregious to conform to the instruction in 3041 (b). In effect, the board has ignored or completely transformed the meaning of "shall normally set a release date" and has transformed the meaning of "shall set a release date unless" to "shall virtually always deny parole because."

The California Supreme Court has upheld most of the board's

---

56 *In re Dannenberg*, pp. 1103–04.
57 Quote from *In re Sandra Davis Lawrence on Habeas Corpus*. Los Angeles County, Superior Court No. A174924, p. 23. In 2002, the Ninth Circuit in *McQuillion v. Duncan* (306 F. 3d 895) found that *Greenholtz* and *Allen* applied to California's sentencing system.

denials or the governor's reversal of a board's decision to grant parole on the basis of unsuitability because of the gravity of the offense as long as there is "some evidence" for considering a particular murder particularly "egregious" or "grave." The Ninth Circuit of the United States Appellate Court in *Biggs v. Terhune* supported the ruling that the decision to deny parole is constitutional if it is supported by "some evidence," but elaborated on the "some evidence" standard:

> The Parole Board's decision is one of "equity" and requires a careful balancing and assessment of the factors considered. As in the present instance, the parole board's sole supportable reliance on the gravity of the offense and conduct prior to imprisonment to justify denial of parole can be initially justified as fulfilling the requirements set forth by state law. Over time, however, should Biggs continue to demonstrate exemplary behavior and evidence of rehabilitation, denying him a parole date simply because of the nature of Biggs' offense and prior conduct would raise serious questions involving his liberty interest in parole.[58]

Other California courts, lower than the California Supreme Court, have specified that "some evidence" must be related to the likelihood that the defendant shall recidivate.[59] In the case of Scott, who was convicted of second degree murder, the court held that:

> The commitment offense can negate suitability only if circumstances of the crime reliably established by evidence in the record rationally indicate that the offender will present an unreasonable public safety risk if released from prison.[60]

More recently, a sentencing court reviewing a habeas petition ruled that the crime cannot be used as an indicator of unsuitability over and over:

> While relying upon petitioner's crime as an indicator of his dangerousness may be reasonable for some period of time—after nearly two decades of incarceration and a half dozen parole suitability hearings—violated due process because petitioner's commitment offense has become such an unreliable predictor of his present and future dangerousness that it does not satisfy the "some evidence" standard. After nearly 20 years of rehabilitation,

---

58 *Biggs v. Terhune*, 334 F. 3d 916–17.
59 *In re Deluna* (2005), 126 Cal. App. 4th 585, 591.
60 *In re Scott* (2005), 133 Cal. App. 4th 573, 595.

the ability to predict a prisoner's future dangerousness based on simply the circumstances of his or her crime is nil.[61]

Finally, another court pointed out that continuing to use the nature of the crime to deny parole is, in effect, converting life with the possibility of parole to life without the possibility of parole:

> Because petitioner cannot change the past, denying petitioner parole based only on the facts surrounding the crime itself effectively changes his sentence from twenty years to life into life without possibility of parole.[62]

At present, the California Board of Prison Terms seems to be influenced by these recent decisions and is setting more parole dates of lifers. However, the governor continues to veto virtually all paroles granted to lifers convicted of homicide and the California Supreme Court continues to back him as they did in the case of Dannenberg. In addition, the governor directly influences the *board's* decisions. In the first place, he appoints all board members. He also removes members when they are seen to have handed out too many paroles to lifers. In 2006, he forced Bilenda Harris-Ritter to resign because she was being criticized by victims' rights organizations for giving out too many paroles:

> Harris-Ritter said she feels she is a casualty in a battle over parole that this year is playing out in the state's courts. For years, she worked to protect victims' rights in her home state of Arkansas before moving to Sacramento. Last year, Gov. Arnold Schwarzenegger appointed her to the state's Board of Parole Hearings. A lawyer and a member of the California Bar Association, Harris-Ritter was thrilled. She said she would bring a crime victim's sensitivity and an attorney's respect for due process to the job. But she'd only been a parole commissioner for a few months before a governor's aide called. Albert Roldan, deputy appointments secretary in Schwarzenegger's office, told her the governor would like her resignation from the board.
>
> She tried to figure out the reason she was let go, and the only thing that made sense, she said, was that a few months earlier she'd seen a web site criticizing her for granting "too many" paroles to prisoners with life sentences.
>
> In the three months she served, Harris-Ritter says she gave only 12 parole grants out of 300 life cases—about four percent. "I

---

61 *Rosenkrantz v. Marshall,* 444 F. Supp. 2d 1084.
62 *Martin v. Marshall,* 431 F. Supp. 2d 1046.

didn't find a public safety reason not to grant them parole and so I followed the law and I granted it," she said.[63]

Another parole board member, Tracey St. Julien, was asked to resign shortly before her Senate confirmation because she was overheard stating that she loved giving parole grants:

> The reason, she said, was that between hearings at the Correctional Training Facility in Soledad a conferencing microphone was accidentally left on. Some district attorneys overheard her casually telling an inmate's lawyer she "loved" giving parole grants. Riverside County prosecutors complained about it in a letter to the board's executive director, while a state group of district attorneys wrote to the governor, St. Julian said.
>
> St. Julian, who said she gave very few grants, defends her eavesdropped statement. "You're dealing with murder," she said. "And if there is any glimmer of hope and humanity . . . then yes, I love that. It didn't happen a lot, but when it happened it was a good feeling. So I made that statement and I would say it again. But apparently it was very unpalatable during the election cycle."[64]

The impact on prisoners and their families of being denied parole year after year when their understanding of the sentencing law indicates that they are eligible for release and they have maintained good conduct in prison and spent years participating in rehabilitative programs is profound. Judge Moody commented on the deleterious impact on lifers and the prison system:

> From the standpoint of the administration of prisons, while the public may not be aware of the realities described above, the inmates most certainly are. The question for them is why, if they are never getting out anyway, should they work, or attend classes, or seek counseling, or abstain from gang activities or stabbings. The mirage of an earned release, followed by the reality of perpetual denials of parole leaves them helpless and extremely embittered. The correctional officers must then face the behavioral consequences.[65]

Lifers who have repeatedly appeared before the board have specific

---

63 Julia Reynolds, "Parole board members feel pressure: Those asked to resign deny that they're soft on crime," *Monterey County Herald*, October 9, 2007.

64 Ibid.

65 Judge Moody, "Commentary."

complaints about its practices. The first is that the hearing, though it is spelled out in the instructions to the board that it should not be, is conducted as a retrying of their offense. And very frequently, the board member who is leading the interrogation of the lifer verbally attacks him:

> I went to the board in 2002 for my IDS [Indeterminate Sentence] date and when I went I remember Wallace was there. No, Wells, Commissioner Wells and someone else and so they told me when I went in, you know, this is not a retrial. This is just a hearing and this hearing is just gonna determine whether or not you're suitable for parole. So when I got in there and everything, we sat down and gave our names and our numbers or whatever. We went through the hearing as if it was a trial. I mean Wells called me everything but—I mean, he called me a dog, that's what he did, you know, when he acknowledged my number he said it "D" as in dog, you know. And I know that in professional etiquette and stuff like we don't do that, you know. And so when he did that I felt like he was personally calling me a dog and so he went through all of my past history stuff and literally told me that I was—he said you was an animal.[66]

> There's a part before the hearing begins that they ask us if we're gonna discuss things today. And if you answer that question yes, they ask you to raise your right hand and take an oath to tell the truth, the whole truth, and nothing but the truth so help you God. You're the only one in that room that takes that oath and I remember that first hearing I didn't even have my hand halfway down and the commissioner slammed both hands on the table and he said so everything you said before this date was a lie? And, I said yeah and it was a lie you know I lied a lot about a lot of things and, so they yelled and they talked to you like a football coach and they would try to press your buttons and try to get you to act out and get angry and throw a tantrum.[67]

Many lifers complain that the board ignores their accomplishments in prison:

> The first time I went to the parole board I'm thinking this is it. They see this. I'm top gun, right? I'm the number one guy there was only nine of us that got the degree out of 6,000 people in San

---

66 Interview, Bobby.
67 Interview, Bryan.

Quentin. So I go in there and I'm really proud of myself and, and do you know they brushed over that with one sentence. Oh we see that you have your Associate Arts degree that's wonderful and you're still attending Alcoholics Anonymous and you're in this cell—brushed it over. Do you know how many days I had to process that. That killed me right there, I mean it killed me it's like I thought I reached the finish line and they just brushed it over with—like it wasn't enough.[68]

In fact, I did a lot better you know I got a lot of stuff, a lot of— went to self-help did all better when I did, when I was found suitable and I come back to the board that next year they denied me a year. I didn't, you know, I didn't understand that. I don't understand the process, you know. They don't have no standard process and how a person can get out. I give them everything. I mean I have a lot of education. I have a home to go home to. My mom, she's a home owner in San Francisco, same house that when I came to prison. Have like six, seven jobs to offer to work, you know, legitimate jobs and I got family support. I've done my time. I have a my sentence is 15 years to life. I've been in prison 28 years and my minimum range parole date is 1990.[69]

After many denials, many lifers become very cynical about the process and see it as "political:"

What's going on is purely politics at work. The politics starts with money, money. It always is. Follow the money and the money, the source of all money for these concerns comes from the prison guards unit, the CCPOA [California Correctional Peace Officers Association] funds a very vulnerable group called the—well groups victims' rights groups it started with the Sharon Tate Victims' crime bureau and Crime Victims' United which is the latter group is solely the family of one victim. A young lady who was murdered by a prisoner, Steve Burns. And that family has managed to take beyond their grief for their loss and gone out and assailed every person in prison and crying that they should never get out because of basically their own personal angst. Now they might run out of steam and out of energy and out of money were it not for the CCPOA who supplies them with six-figure contributions to do such dirty work as running TV ads in the central valley

---

68 Interview, Bryan.
69 Interview, German.

against the amendment of the three strikes law, for example that was in the last election.[70]

I got 30 years in. This is my thirtieth year, so at 25 to life, I was eligible at 15 years. You're eligible for parole, so I still would have been able, I have four times my eligibility in now, over four times my eligibility on the 7 to life. So and the thing is that I think, you know, we've just been caught up in the politics, the political game, where each governor and each legislator has decided that it was more politically safe to lock us up and throw away the key. It's just the routine now. Now Mr. Morris we're here for your thirteenth board hearing today. This is commissioner wop-wop and this is commissioner so-and-so and today we're gonna be discussing your subsequent parole hearing and we're gonna be discussing your suitability for parole and that's how it starts off and then they just go through this ABC process, you know, review my record, what I got arrested for, what I was sentenced to, how much time, review my disciplinary, how long I've been down, what part disciplinary history I've had since I've been incarcerated, review my in-custody progress, you know, what I got in education then receiving an education, trade all the things, you know, self-help programs, all the things you're expected to do while you're in prison. Then they hear from the victims, hear from the district attorney, hear from me, hear from my attorney and then that's it. That's the basic form of parole hearing and then they make a decision, send you out of the room. OK Mr. Morris, this time we're gonna make our decision. You go, anywhere from 30 minutes to an hour depending on how much debate they go through or discussion and then you're brought back in and, at least in my case, I'm brought back in and I'm told at this time we find you unsuitable and it's for the following reasons. And it's always the same reason. That's the thing that I was saying earlier. It is that of the crime, it's past behavior then that's it for me and then they'll throw something in like continuing to improve your education or continue vocational upgrades or stay disciplinary free. That's a real big deal they keep throwing out there all the time. Stay disciplinary free. Once they make a decision there's no opportunity for discourse, you know, we made the decision that's it.[71]

70 Interview, Dannenberg.
71 Interview, Lonnie.

You know I'm going to the board. After you get sentenced to 25 to life, 15 to life, they set your minimum term. Fifteen to lifers go to the board in 10 years, 25 to life go in 15, 17 years. The regulation states that the board shall normally set a parole date. However, they never do. They normally deny you. And what happens is you're not aware what's going on. The society or politics, that's going on. You will probably do the rest of your life in prison because a game going on now. They're using the hard on crime for political gain. So whoever's harder on crime is the one getting elected. They violate their own laws just to get elected. So a prisoner like me, if we don't learn the law, we going to do the rest of our lives in prison. In my case, I don't believe that I should still be in prison. I should've been out for over 10 years and I'm still here.[72]

In expressing their punitiveness and guarding against possible negative reaction from the public for releasing a criminal, the governor and the judges are ignoring two serious problems. The first is the expense of caring for the growing number of lifers who are serving excessively long sentences, many of whom are moving into advanced ages and are requiring more and more expensive medical care. The medical care functions of the California Department of Corrections and Rehabilitation are already in control of a "Receiver" appointed by a Northern California District Federal Judge, which in itself is costing the state millions of dollars. The cost of caring for aging lifers will soar into millions more in the future.

The second problem is the inhumanity of holding persons who, though they committed a serious crime, sometimes a horrible crime, have, through the years, matured into completely different human beings than the "offenders" they were many years, perhaps two or three decades, ago. Most of these individuals not only experience the normal process of maturation through which immature, irresponsible, conscienceless, often psychologically disturbed, and socially dislocated young people "grow up." But they also, through the imprisonment experience, gain insight and remorse, and vigorously participate in programs to improve themselves. When citizens meet a lifer who has served 15 to 30 years, they are usually overwhelmed by their recognition that this person is not only an ordinary, but often an admirable human being.

---

72 Interview, Noel.

7

EPILOGUE

CRACKS IN THE DAM

A dramatic change in the legal situation of California lifers is occurring. The U.S. Federal Courts have been vacating the denials of parole based on the lifers' crime or their pre-conviction behavior as "some evidence" that their release represents an unreasonable risk to public safety. In earlier cases, *Biggs v. Terhune* and *Irons v. Carey*,[73] Federal Courts held that the crime loses its power to be a predictor of future dangerousness as the prisoner serves more time. In recent years, California Courts, particularly the California Court of Appeals for the 4th District, have been ruling in cases in which the prisoner has served more than their minimum sentence that the crime alone is not a sufficient factor in establishing that the individual is a danger to public safety.[74] Most recently, in the case of *In re Sandra Davis Lawrence*, the Court of Appeals of the State of California, 2nd District, vacated the governor's reversal of the Board of Prison Terms (BPT)'s fourth recommendation that Lawrence be released on parole. The governor had used Lawrence's crime as his main reason for reversing the parole board's decision. He wrote, "But as stated in my 2004 decision, the murder perpetrated by Ms. Lawrence demonstrated a shockingly vicious use of lethality and an exceptionally callous disregard for human suffering because after she shot Mrs. Williams—four times—causing her to collapse to the floor,

---

73 *Biggs v. Terhune* (9th Cir. 2003) 334 F. 3d and *Irons v. Carey* (9th Cir. 2007) 479 F. 3d.
74 See *In re Smith* (2003) 109 Cal. App. 4th, *In re Scott* (2004) 109 Cal. App. 4th, and *In re Lee* (2005) 143 Cal. App. 4th.

Ms. Lawrence stabbed her repeatedly."[75] The court disagreed with the governor's characterization of her crime and her lack of remorse, and decided that "Lawrence's commitment offense, now over 30 years in the past and after nearly a quarter century of incarceration, does not provide 'some evidence' her present release would represent an 'unreasonable risk' of danger to the community."[76]

In 2008, the United States Court of Appeals for the Ninth Circuit in the case of *Ronald Hayward v. John Marshall* vacated the governor's reversal of the decision of the BPT in granting Hayward a parole *and* the Los Angeles Court's decision to uphold the governor's reversal. They stated:

> Hayward was initially sentenced to a term of fifteen years to life in prison. Hayward has been in prison for twenty-seven years. In *Irons*, we noted that in all the cases in which we have held that a parole board's decision to deem a prisoner unsuitable for parole solely on the basis of his commitment offense comports with due process, the decision was made before the inmate had served the minimum number of years required by his sentence. Specifically, in *Biggs, Sass*, and here, [in *Irons*] the petitioner had not served the minimum number of years to which they had been sentenced at the time of the challenged parole denial by the Board.
>
> Therefore, we concluded that "all we held in those cases and all we hold today is that, given the particular circumstances of the offenses in these cases, due process was not violated when these prisoners were deemed unsuitable for parole prior to the expiration of their minimum terms." Here by contrast, Hayward has long served more than his minimum fifteen-year term of imprisonment. We hold that the Governor's reversal of parole in this case was not supported by any evidence that Hayward's release would threaten public safety, and that the Governor's reversal of his parole thus violated his due process rights.[77]

It appears that the dam that has held back the release of thousands of lifers who have served many years over the time prescribed by PC 3041 and the Administrative Code that established the appropriate sentences for first and second degree homicide is finally cracking. Since Hayward, many lifers have had their Habeas Corpus petitions accepted by the

---

75 *In re Sandra Davis Lawrence*, Cal. App. 2nd 16.
76 Ibid., p. 31.
77 *Ronald Hayward v. John Marshall* (9th Cir. 2008) 512 F. 3d 536, 29–30.

Federal Courts. In the months to come, a flood of lifers may leave California prisons and enter free society. Though there is considerable evidence that this will not represent a problem to public safety, it does pose a tremendous problem of "reentry" for the lifers themselves.

REENTRY

The problem of prisoner reentry has reached enormous proportions. In 2002, approximately 600,000 persons were released from America's prisons. Today, the number is probably over 700,000. City, state, and the federal governments now recognize the enormity of the problem and are mounting some efforts to address it. In the spring of 2008, the Federal Government passed "Second Chance" that allocates $165 million annually for reentry programs. However, these measures are underfunded and do not address the full scope of the problems returning prisoners face.

The Reentry Problem in General

Lifers' difficulties in adjusting to the outside world are the most severe, but all prisoners confront great difficulties when they leave prison. The first of these is just "getting settled down." To accomplish this they must first withstand the initial impact of living on the outside. They have been acculturated to prison life with its slower pace, monotony, strict regulation, routinization, and reduced stimulus.[78] They step into a world with fast moving cars, buses, tall buildings, swarming crowds, hoards of women, kids running around, animal pets, bright lights, strange noises and smells, all of which they have not encountered, perhaps for many years. In addition, they have lost most or many of the automatic responses that equip citizens to perform everyday transactions—getting on a bus, paying the fare, making change, talking to strangers whose accent or vernacular is different from theirs, ordering food at a food stand or restaurant, crossing a busy street, and riding in an automobile. They are, in effect, strangers in a strange land.

The effect of this is to jar them out of kilter. They become confused, disoriented, and depressed. Frequently, this alone incapacitates them, diverts them from their planned courses of action, and ushers them

---

78 In the 1930s, Donald Clemmer, the father of sociology of the prison, described how "prisonization" assimilates prisoners into the culture of the prison. In his words: "we may use the term *Prisonization* to indicate the taking on in greater or less degree of the folkways, mores, customs, and general culture of the penitentiary." *The Prison Community* (New York: Holt, Rinehart and Winston, 1940), p. 299.

back into deviant behavior, such as drug use. This confusion and other effects of being a stranger in a strange land will last for at least several days, sometimes several weeks.

Once they withstand this initial impact, they must fulfill the exigencies of living in a free society. First of all, they must locate a place to live—no small feat in contemporary society with its extreme lack of low rent residences. Ex-prisoners' difficulty in finding housing is reflected in the fact that nearly half remain homeless.[79]

They must find work. Unless they have some established employment possibility, such as union membership, a job waiting for them, or a highly marketable skill, they are at an extreme disadvantage. They are society's least employable class of people seeking jobs. They have a "record." Most of them are non-white. Most are not trained in an occupation that is hiring new employees. They lack a history of stable employment. Or at least, they have a big gap in their employment record. A California Department of Correction's study found that 70 percent of the parolees released between July 1996 and June 1997 were unemployed in each quarter of that year. The percentage is probably as high or higher today.

Finally, they must acquire all the accoutrements required for living in a free society: clothing, tools, furnishings, toiletries, picture ID, driver's license, and means of transportation. They are starting from scratch. Typically, they have very limited funds. As I suggested in an earlier study, "Most prisoners step into the outside world with a small bundle of stuff under their arm, a little bit of money, perhaps their $200 'gate' money, and that's all."[80]

Dealing with Parole

Most prisoners are released on parole supervision and this is another obstacle they must cross. Though in earlier eras, parole was intended to be a mixture of helping and policing services, parole supervision in California has become mainly a policing enterprise. This is reflected in the extremely high rate of return of California parolees to prisons—by far the highest in the country. Approximately 70% of prisoners released from California prisons return within the first two years, more than half of them for violation of the conditions of parole. (Most states have a return rate of less than 50%.) Most "violators," that is, persons who are sent back to prison for violation of the conditions of parole, are

---

79 Amanda Ripley in an article in *Time* reports that "30% to 50% of big-city parolees are homeless" (*Time*, January 21, 2002, pp. 58–62).

80 Irwin, *The Warehouse Prison*, p. 174.

charged with "dirty urines" (urines that test positive for drugs), and failure to make contact with their parole agent.

The California parole agency shifted to a more punitive approach to parole supervision for many reasons. First, they are following the lead of the last few California governors who have all been "tough on crime." This trend started with George Deukmejian (1983–91) who established a policy of "tail 'em and nail 'em," that is, supervise them closely and charge them with any infraction of the conditions of parole. It continued with Pete Wilson (1991–99), and then Gray Davis (1999–2003), both of whom were conservative on the issue of crime. Arnold Schwarzenegger (2003), who began his term promising to reduce prison populations, instructed the parole division to stop sending so many parolees back to prison. This precipitated a strong reaction from the guards' union and victims' rights organizations. Schwarzenegger backed off and began his own "tough on crime" policies.

Second, the parole agency, like other policing organizations, such as city police departments, have a built-in tendency to become conservative and punitive. This is because they deal directly with the problems of mostly lower-class citizens, many of whom behave in a bothersome, deviant, even threatening manner. Parole agents' primary assignment is that of keeping these irksome troublemakers under control. In addition, parole agents have been expected to help parolees adjust to outside society and to establish themselves in a conventional, non-criminal permanent adjustment. The problem is they lack the resources to accomplish this. Parole agencies have very limited funds to aid parolees who are in need of immediate financial assistance for things such as rent, food, tools, prescription drugs, and transportation. They have a few contacts, mostly with other agencies that find employment for parolees, to which they refer parolees. The tendency is for agents to become cynical and critical of the parolees, many of whom are beseeching them for assistance or causing them extra work in trying to track them.

Helping Agencies

The CDCR has job counselors at the various district parole offices. These counselors hold workshops and work individually with parolees who seek their services. The state and federal governments fund several job placement offices, such as One Stop and Work Place. Private organizations, particularly some churches, have established job placement programs for ex-prisoners. It was my observation when I studied these programs in my research on the "warehouse prison" that these programs do three things:

First, they refer ex-prisoners to minimum-wage jobs, usually less than full time, at various retail businesses, car washes, warehouses, and janitorial services. Second, they conduct regular workshops where there is some job referral and, more important, a great deal of motivational support. The message the program staff delivers, frequently with considerable enthusiasm and eloquence, is, "You can make it if you don't give up." Third, and perhaps most important, these programs created many jobs *in* the programs. Most of the program staff themselves, often the directors, are ex-convicts. These persons are making a better salary than most employed ex-prisoners and are performing work they enjoy and believe is valuable. In effect, they have careers. This type of career is very popular among prisoners and ex-prisoners.[81]

Doing Good

If they establish an economically viable life on the outside, most ex-prisoners desire to move on and fulfill their aspirations of achieving a higher standard of living. They want to "do good." That is, they want to get a *good* job and put together a non-criminal, stable, more or less rewarding life on the outside. Doing good involves having a job with a "living wage," security, and job satisfaction. It involves a suitable residence, rewarding friendships, and perhaps marriage, a home, and a family. These are difficult to achieve because of ex-prisoners' debilitating prison experiences and their ex-convict stigma. Only a very small percentage achieve the level of doing good.

Failure

In California, most ex-prisoners (70 percent) are sent back to prison. Most of those who are not sent back to prison still fail to achieve the standard of living, the satisfactions, or the fulfillments they aspired to when they were in prison making plans about their life after prison. Many drift on the edge, crossing back and forth inside and outside the law and the parole rules. They occasionally work low-wage jobs, hustle some, lay low, keep away from their parole agents, and try to keep their life together and avoid being arrested or "violated" by their parole agents. Others descend into a life of dependency and live off their spouses or parents or draw Supplemental Security Income. Tragically, many become derelicts and gravitate to the world of the homeless street people who live day to day, drinking,

81 Ibid., p. 178.

hanging out, and surviving by making the rounds of soup kitchens and homeless shelters. A study of homeless persons in New York in the 1990s revealed that 80 percent of the homeless had been in jail, prison, or a mental hospital.[82] A Los Angeles police captain, who had participated in a "sweep" of LA's skid row in 2002, remarked, "The area has the highest concentration of parolees in the state, almost 2000."[83]

Lifers' Reentry

All of a sudden one day you're free, and you are told to go back into society and function the best way that you can. Well, that best way I can is not good enough because I now have a criminal history that I didn't have before. I don't have an education needed to apply for a job that's worthwhile having. I don't have the funds needed to pay for basic necessities such as clothing, housing, food, transportation.[84]

Lifers' return to the outside world is different because of the lengthy sentence they served. In California, the vast majority have been locked up for more than 20 years, most of them, more than 25 years. They have become more thoroughly acculturated to the prison world. In the 20 plus years they were away, things outside have changed dramatically, particularly changes driven by electronic technology. In every public place, many or most people circulate while plugged into their iPods, talking or sending text messages on cell phones, or, with a little bug-like apparatus stuck in their ears, seemingly talking to nobody, just talking. In the ubiquitous, tony coffee shops, people sit around drinking coffee and reading or working on their laptops. Gigantic malls abound. Shopping is way of life. The array of products on display is huge and overwhelming. Prices have tripled. People pour out of wholesale outlets like Cosco, Home Depot, Office Depot, Best Buy with cart-loads of purchases. Everyone is busier, walking faster and zooming around in their convertibles, Hummers, high powered pickups, or racy sport cars. Traffic has more than doubled. The strangeness of the outside world is more confusing for released lifers than for other releasees who served shorter sentences. For example, Michael Anthony Williams takes a

---

82 Martha Burt, *Over the Edge* (New York: Urban Institute and Russell Sage, 1992).

83 Quoted in Andrew Blankstein and Richard Winton, "130 Arrested In Sweep of Skid Row," *Los Angeles Times*, November 21, 2002, p. B12.

84 Herman Atkins quoted from "Exonerated Prisoners," in *Religion & Ethics NewsWeekly*, July 22, 2007. This is a story of a lifer whose conviction was overturned. In the last few years, there have been many follow-up interviews of exonerated prisoners who are increasing in numbers and receiving media attention.

driver's test soon after his release from Angola, the Louisiana State Prison:

> As so often happens lately, Michael Anthony Williams is lost. The driver's license examiner towers over him, rattling off orders through the rolled-down window on the driver's side. But at each command, Williams, 40, hesitates. He signals to the left when he is told to turn right. He forgets to turn off the windshield wipers. He fails the test, another blow in Williams' quest to put together a life that was taken from him when he was just a boy. At the age of 16, a sophomore in Jonesboro High School in northern Louisiana, he was arrested and convicted of raping his female math tutor. He spent 24 years in the Angola state penitentiary. Two months ago, he walked free.[85]

Lifers have aged significantly. Most of them came to prison in their late teens or early twenties. They will be at least over 40 when they leave prison. Many will be in their fifties or sixties. Their employability is greatly reduced by this.

However, lifers have received much more vocational training than other prisoners. They had more time to participate in vocational programs. But also, they were much more motivated to attend these programs. Part of this motivation comes from their trying to present evidence of their rehabilitation to the parole board, but it also comes from their sincere desire to prepare themselves for life after prison. The lifers I interviewed indicated that they had participated in two or three of the following programs: sheet metal, welding, plumbing, shoe repair, dry cleaning, and computer repair.

However, most of the vocational training programs in California prisons do not adequately prepare persons for employment in the trade on the outside or prepare them for jobs for which they have a good chance of being hired because they require union membership, which in most cases is difficult to acquire. Three that do prepare persons for outside jobs are sheet metal, plumbing, and welding.

Most of the lifers in my sample have outside support from families with whom they have kept close contact or have re-united. Seven are married. Four got married while they were in prison. Before 1990, they could have conjugal visits and a few have children born while they were in prison. These family ties will be very important in their reentry.

Many of the lifers in San Quentin have established close ties with

---

85 Anna Badkhen, "Rough Landing for Exonerated Inmate," *San Francisco Chronicle*, May 9, 2005.

various outside public service programs and churches through which they find employment upon release. For example, many of the lifers who participated in IMPACT (Incarcerated Men Putting Away Childish Things) in San Quentin went out to good jobs. One is in the sheet metal workers' union and another in the plumbers' union. Three of them are working for IMPACT, which is now funded by CDCR, and are teaching the principles of the program in Youth Authority prisons.

Five of the sample of lifers I interviewed have been released. Bryan was released a year ago and is presently getting by very well. He is working for Full Circle Addiction Services, a non-profit private organization with which he was associated before he was released. He regularly speaks on drug addiction and recovery at conferences, colleges, and treatment centers. He has a small apartment and gets around the East Bay on BART (Bay Area Rapid Transit). He has found that things like clothes are very expensive, but he is living cautiously and frugally. He is currently making plans to attend college, which was his expressed intention when I interviewed him in prison.

German was released in the fall of 2007 after serving 27 years. He is married and lives with his mother. He is a counselor at the Bernal Heights Neighborhood Center. He intends to enroll at San Francisco State University.

Julius was picked up by Immigration upon his release. He was a legal non-citizen when he was arrested, but the new policy after the passage of the Patriot Act is to deport non-citizens who have been convicted of a serious felony. He is currently fighting his deportation.

Rachman was released from the LA county jail after the judge threw out his conviction and the prosecutor's office declined to retry him. He was married while he was in prison and now has children. He is living in Fresno, California with his wife. In September 2008, he was the keynote speaker at the annual graduation ceremonies at San Quentin. His prospects for a successful life seem to be good.

Prospects for the Future

If the trickle of lifers coming out of prison turns into a flood, it is not certain they will have the same success as the lifers described above. Many of the latter obtained employment with public service organizations that address problems of delinquency, crime, and drug addiction. These persons had considerable life experience and in-prison training preparing them for this type of work. However, the number of positions in these fields is limited and the existing organizations will not be able to absorb hundreds of lifers. Nor will the few unions, such as the plumbers', sheet metal, and welders' unions, absorb the flood.

To avoid the tragic eventuality of hundreds of released lifers living out a life of impecunious dependency, homelessness, or life on skid row, a large investment in special reentry programs will be required. Programs like IMPACT serve as a model for lifer reentry programs. An effective program should have a significant "inside" phase in which prisoners spend considerable time in preparation for release. This would include developing insights into the attitudes, habits, and propensities that led to their crimes; learning the skills that will be required to operate in the free society; and making concrete arrangements for living outside. In addition, an effective reentry program should have an intense mentoring/counseling operation that assists the newly released prisoner in his or her transition to the outside. Finally, there should be a substantial follow-up capacity to assist ex-prisoners over the persistent series of obstacles they encounter and for which they have limited experience and resources to aid them.

For two important reasons, prisoners and ex-prisoners should have a major part in the planning, administration, and execution of these programs. The first reason is that prisoners and ex-prisoners have special knowledge of the problems of preparing for and actually passing through reentry. (It must be noted that most of the self-help programs at San Quentin, such as IMPACT, were created and maintained by prisoners themselves.) The second reason is that many lifers have been preparing themselves for public service careers related to crime, delinquency, and drug abuse and this would open up new employment possibilities for them.

Funding these programs will require a large investment of public money. However, when compared to the extreme expenses involved in supervising ex-prisoners on parole and that of their re-incarceration, which is in excess of $4,000 a month per person, adequately funded reentry programs would actually save money.

CONCLUSION

The major theme of this book has been that lifers, though they have committed the most serious crime, homicide, can be transformed through the years in prison into decent, responsible, caring human beings. A second theme has been that, during the current punitive era that has dominated criminal justice policy for the last several decades, they are being held in prison many years more than is called for by the stated goals of imprisonment and the dictates of the law. This unjust, apparently illegal, and certainly counterproductive treatment of these persons reflects something very disturbing about our society. A crucial test of a society's humanity is the manner in which it treats its least advantaged members—the poor, the sick, and the mentally ill. As has been suggested (either by George Bernard Shaw or Fyodor Dostoyevsky, perhaps both), the *ultimate* test is the manner in which it treats its prisoners. America is failing on this measure. The millions of poor people, the worst medical delivery system among modern nations, the mistreatment of the mentally ill, and our bloated prison population testify to this failure.

The usual justification for the prolonged imprisonment of lifers is that their crimes are so egregious they do not deserve forgiveness, kindness, or even fairness under the law. They are repudiated pariah. Many, perhaps most, citizens hold this belief because they have accepted a false dichotomy: that the world is divided into good people and bad people. In upholding this distinction, they ignore the sins and serious crimes of good people (and often, their own). Almost every day, the business pages report a new round of indictments of stock brokers, financial managers, and other financial professionals for crimes involving millions of dollars, many of which have resulted in the loss of the life savings of hundreds of thousands of ordinary people (Enron comes to mind.) Or we hear that the top officials in the government planned and ordered the torture of persons held as "enemy combatants." Or that some of our soldiers, our best young men, while overseas protecting democracy, assassinated civilians. Most of these "good people," even if convicted of crimes, are forgiven, given light sentences, and often pardoned. The dichotomy doesn't hold up to close examination. The saying "there but by twists of fate go I" applies.

The conservative ideology that underpins this good-and-evil-people belief also excites citizens' desire for revenge. The effects of the widespread expression of vengeance are pernicious, both to the society and to the individual seeking it. It divides us and leads to the adoption of policies, such as massive imprisonment, that exacerbate many social problems. Low-income families and their communities are damaged; children are raised in fatherless homes or, in a growing number of cases, separated from their mothers; restorative measures to bring victims and offenders together are discouraged; and the victims of crimes are consumed by the belief that offenders have not been punished enough, which adds to victims' pain.[86]

---

86 The victims' rights movement, which has greatly interfered with the rational delivery of punishment, is a manifestation of this unfulfilled desire for revenge.

INDEX